The First
TEE SHOT

The First
TEE SHOT

A Parent's Guide to Teaching Kids Golf

WALLY ARMSTRONG

WITH MIKE YORKEY

BROADMAN
&HOLMAN
PUBLISHERS

NASHVILLE, TENNESSEE

0-8054-3128-4

Published by Broadman & Holman Publishers,
Nashville, Tennessee

Dewey Decimal Classification: 248.82
Subject Heading: GOLF \ CHRISTIAN LIFE \ BIBLE—STUDY

Published in association with the literary agency of Alive Communications, Inc.,
7680 Goddard Street, Suite 200, Colorado Springs, Colorado 80920

Scripture quotations are taken from:
The Holman Christian Standard Bible® (HCSB),
© 1999, 2000, 2002, 2003 Holman Bible Publishers.
The Holy Bible, New International Version (NIV),
© 1973, 1978, 1984 by International Bible Society.
The Holy Bible, New Living Translation (NLT),
© 1996, used by permission of Tyndale House Publishers, Inc.,
Wheaton, Illinois 60189, all rights reserved.

1 2 3 4 5 6 7 8 9 10 08 07 06 05 04

"Golf, like measles, should be caught young,
for if postponed to riper years, the results may be serious."

—P. G. WODEHOUSE
from *The Golf Omnibus*

CONTENTS

INTRODUCTION

Let's pretend it's Saturday morning, a period of quality time for you and your two children, ages nine and six. You enjoy playing golf, but you only tee it up ten times a year because five-hour rounds take too much time away from the family—and Sundays are jam-packed with church and other worthy activities anyway. This morning, your oldest child, Josh, reads about Tiger Woods in *Sports Illustrated for Kids,* and he asks if he can play golf with you.

"Why, sure . . . I'd love to," you stammer. Six-year-old Heather, who overhears the conversation, chimes in, "Me too, me too!" She doesn't want to be left out.

Now you're standing on rubberized mats at the local driving range with a large bucket in your hand. You drop a dozen or so balls into their hitting stations and stand back. Josh, a third grader who's a terror on the Little League diamond, takes a mighty cut at the stationary ball and whiffs it. He flails several more times before topping the ball twenty yards. Josh looks pretty frustrated.

Heather, meanwhile, isn't sure what to do. She awkwardly grips an oversized junior driver, but the implement feels strange in her hands. She attempts several halfhearted swings, but she fails to put the clubface on the ball.

"I can't hit it," she whines. "I hate this game."

Josh puts his hands on hips. "I'm not having fun either," he declares. "Can we go home?"

What do you do?

A. Tell them: "Forget it. You're just getting started. Did you think this game would be easy? Keep trying!"

B. Get your clubs and spend the next fifteen minutes working on your long irons.

C. Tell them: "You think Tiger Woods was knocking it three hundred yards the first time he tried golf? You'll never hit it like him if you quit now."

D. Pick up the balls and take the kids out for an ice cream.

The correct answer is *D*. Sure, you may have to leave behind a bunch of balls for others to hit (unless you ask for a refund in the pro shop), but you want to be thinking long term, and your long-term goal is making golf fun for your kids. If you turn them off the first time, you risk turning them off forever.

So, how can you get your kids into a wonderful sport that they can enjoy for a lifetime—and play with you for many years? And what type of spiritual lessons does golf teach us about the way we should act and the way we should play?

You'll find the answers in this book specifically written for you—the parent of children three to eighteen years old who's looking for contagious ways to infect your kids with the great game of golf while imparting a spiritual lesson or two along the way. I bring years of hands-on experience to the driving range. Not only am I a lifetime member of the Professional Golfers' Association (PGA), but I'm also the father of three children, two of whom are young adults and another nearing the end of his teen years: Dana is twenty-nine years old; Scott is twenty-six; and Blake is eighteen.

I introduced golf to all three of my kids, and each outcome has been different. Dana, for instance, hasn't picked up a club in years; she is married and recently gave birth to our first grandchild, so her interests lie elsewhere. Scott, who recently married, is gung ho about golf and has turned that passion into a budding television career with PGA Tour productions. Blake, my youngest, is attending a junior college and plays in a band. He's a noncompetitive teen with a half-dozen activities and interests vying for his attention; golf is only one of them.

Let me hasten to add that there is no *right* outcome regarding golf and your children. Every child is different: some will instantly love hitting balls and clamor to hit more; others will find the sport as boring as watching grass grow. That's OK. Golf is not a fast-moving game like the action-oriented sports of football, basketball, soccer, and hockey. It's not a team sport either (except in high school and college). But golf is a challenging game that mirrors the ups and downs of life, a game that constantly renews itself. Golf is a wonderful sport played on beautiful, well-manicured grounds that inspire our souls. Whether you've never hit a ball in anger or if you've been hooked by the sport for years, this book will help *you* introduce your children to the basics of golf, including how to swing a club, golf etiquette, and how to play a round of golf.

Golf is also one of the best games I know that teaches us how God wants us to act. "Our character is what we do when we think no one is looking," author H. Jackson Brown Jr., once said, which applies perfectly to golf because golf is an honorable game where you're expected to be your own judge and jury regarding rules infractions. There is no umpire or referee hovering nearby to make sure you don't break a rule or commit a foul. It is a common occurrence, at all levels of golf, for a player to own up to the slightest breach of the Rules of Golf that no one else witnessed. Sure, some people cheat, but God sees it.

The concept that you call rule infractions on yourself is a difficult one to accept—or teach—in today's postmodern culture, which says that no one has a monopoly on truth. The thinking goes like this: If you think you have a five on a hole when you really had a six, then you had a five because that's true to you. Golf, on the other hand, is a game of absolutes—you either had a five or a six. The ball is either in bounds or it isn't. If it took you three swings to get out of the bunker, then it took you three swings. A four-putt is a four-putt.

Golf is also a game that teaches that you are responsible for your actions and your own shot-playing; you can't blame someone else for a poor shot (although countless millions have tried). Similarly, we will all be responsible for our past actions when we stand before

---

If You're a Single-Parent Mom . . .

. . . then know this book is for you. While it may seem *The First Tee Shot* is directed to fathers, I want to assure married moms and single-parent moms that you don't have to be knowledgeable about golf to get your kids involved in the sport. Even if you haven't played much, you can use *The First Tee Shot* to learn golf together—and teach a few biblical lessons along the way.

Another thing you should know is that hundreds of collegiate golf scholarships for young women go unused each year. If your daughter is a good athlete and gets bitten by the golf bug, she could bag a scholarship to a fine school. All it takes is lots of practice and a mind-set that she can do it.

God on Judgment Day, when "each of us will give an account of himself to God" (Rom. 14:12 HCSB).

Playing golf with your children will give you ample opportunities to teach them about absolute truth. When your children watch you walk back to the tee box after you discover that your tee shot hit a cart path and bounced out of bounds, they'll remember that. Not only do they notice those little things, but they will be listening to what you say during a round. (So watch your language!)

It's All about Relationship

Think about it: What other sport gives you a captive audience with your kids for four or five hours? What other sport presents so much concentrated time to interact with your children? Hunting, perhaps, and you could make an argument for skiing or snowboarding, but I've long felt that golf is the *best* sporting activity that parents can do with their children.

The bull's-eye of *The First Tee Shot* is to deepen your relationship with your kids, and golf happens to be a means to that end. This is what I call *real* target golf. Mark Twain once said that golf is a "good walk spoiled," but don't tell that to a mother or father who just finished strolling down the eighteenth fairway with their children on a sunny afternoon. If you don't agree, then ask anyone who's lost a parent what they would give to enjoy another leisurely round with their loved one.

Let me say another thing about relationship. Golf can help you cement your relationship with your children, as long as you don't force the sport down their throats or have a "here's what we're going to do today, Johnny" agenda at the driving range. How you act and what you say will determine if you have a golfing buddy in the future or someone who runs away from the sport. You can't force your kids to play golf, just as you can't force your children to faith—you can only instill spiritual values and point your children toward Christ. All children have a free will, and that plays a big part in whether they choose to follow what they've been taught about God and about golf.

That's why your kids need to know that if they top the ball into a canyon or four-putt from fifteen feet, you'll be there to pick them up, pat them on their backsides, and send them to the next tee box. If they're discouraged, then you're the first to encourage. If they're having fun, then you'll have fun with them—even if you're having a lousy day on the course. Believe me, the score you write on your scorecard is the least important result of the day!

Allow Me to Introduce Myself

You may be wondering what credentials—besides being the father of three children—qualify me to write this book. I have been playing golf for most of my life. I grew up in the cornfields of Indiana and caddied and played in junior golf tournaments. My dad took me to Fort Benjamin Harrison Golf Club for lessons, and I can still remember my first session with Fred Keesling, the golf professional at the club. I had a baseball grip that produced a huge unnecessary dip in my swing. Fred explained the importance of having a good grip, and as he placed his huge hands over mine, he molded them into the correct grip, which has become the foundation of my swing for more than fifty years.

I was fortunate to win the Indiana State High School Championship before playing collegiate golf at the University of Florida. Following graduation, I completed my master's degree in health and human performance at Florida, and then I spent a short stint caddying on the PGA Tour for a childhood idol, Gary Player. Through the encouragement of Gary and other friends, I pursued playing on the PGA Tour and found myself ten years later playing a practice round with Gary himself at the Masters in Augusta, Georgia.

Although I never won a PGA event, I finished second four times and led in more than thirty-one tournaments, which included being on top for a few holes during the third round of my first Masters. During my eleven years on the Tour, I competed in more than three hundred events, and because of my record and accomplishments, I was awarded a lifetime membership to the PGA Tour.

Many people do not know this, but I saw myself more as a golf evangelist on the Tour than as a player. I shared my faith and story with anyone and any group who would listen. I had the privilege of helping conduct the weekly PGA Tour Chapels. It was such a blessing to be able to have one-on-one conversations with

PGA pros, tour officials, tournament volunteers, and many of the thousands of spectators I met throughout my career. Always, my goal was to spread the good news of God's love—not win titles—although I very much wanted to win because that would have increased my platform.

Once I left the PGA Tour, I began a successful golf teaching career that has allowed me to conduct clinics in all fifty states and twenty countries. I have done hundreds of clinics for junior golfers, and many of these were done with my own

two sons, Scott and Blake. Because of my love for kids and my desire to have parents learn how to help their kids get into the game of golf, in 1986 with my ten-year-old son Scott, I produced "Golf for Kids of All Ages," my first instructional tape. For parents and kids, this video has been distributed worldwide from the U.S. to Europe to Japan. Then when our other son, Blake, was nine years old, he was the main instructor in another tape we produced. It contains some unique interviews with Blake and PGA Tour stars like Tom Lehman, Brad Faxon, and Billy Andrade. As you can see from this unique book in your hands, these two golf instructional videos are included on a DVD for your use.

INTRODUCTION

One of the highlights of my teaching career was to conduct a junior clinic at the Tournament Players Club (TPC) in Scottsdale, Arizona. This clinic was done with my son Scott, along with former Vice President Dan Quayle, forty-one local golf professionals, two touring golf professionals, and three hundred kids and parents. As I was introduced by the head golf professional, he referred to me as the "world's oldest junior golfer." From that moment on I knew "who I was," and that's one of the main reasons I am so thrilled to be able to get this book into your hands. Harvey Penick always referred to himself as a grown caddy. One of your greatest assets as a parent working with your child is to let out the little kid inside you.

But enough about me. I am concerned about you and your children. I want you and your kids to fall in love with a great game—a game that will provide you with scores of "mentoring moments."

Golf is also a game that gives you fairway-wide opportunities to share your faith. Think about it: other than on a golf course when and where would you have a better opportunity to talk with your children or friends about how God changed your life or what God is teaching you? Golf has those one-on-one quiet moments that allow reflection and sharing one's thoughts, hopes, and dreams. It would be pretty difficult to share your faith in the midst of a pickup basketball game or some other team sport.

That's because golf is a relational sport that bonds participants; it doesn't pull them apart. Just as evangelism works best when it's relational—when you listen, carry on a conversation, and empathize—doors can open on a golf course that are slammed shut anywhere else.

One final thought on sharing your faith on the golf course: be patient. Playing golf builds friendships and relationships, and it may be that *after* the round your child or friend feels comfortable enough to open up to you, giving you a wide-open chance to talk about how Christ has changed your life.

Well, are you ready to get started? Good, because I think they're calling our names at the first tee right now. . . .

1

WHY GOLF IS
A GREAT GAME

When my son Scott was six years old, he loved accompanying me to the driving range and whacking ball after ball. If I emptied a big yellow bucket, then he matched me swing for swing.

I was happy that Scott relished hitting range balls, but something inside me said, *Don't push him*, so I did my best to avoid becoming the Golf Parent from Hell. Whenever I saw his interest waning, I would call it quits and hand him some change for the Coke machine.

About that time an old college roommate, Joe Prochaska, gave me a call. Joe told me his son, Bard (a year younger than Scott), was starting to play golf as well. "What do you say we have a father-son golf outing?" Joe suggested.

"Sounds great, Joe. There's a new junior chip-and-putt course at Disney World that would be perfect for the boys," I said. "The holes are 75 to 150 yards long; there's plenty of room, almost no sand bunkers—it would be just perfect for the kids."

While Scott had played a few holes with me, this would be the first time he would play a "real" golf course. Of course, I wanted him to come off the eighteenth green raving about what a good time he had, but I also wanted him to learn more about golf. The last time we played a couple of holes together, I noticed that he would advance the ball in little chips toward the green until he poked the ball *barely* on the green. Then he would start jabbing dinky putts in the direction of the hole. The thought of actually hitting the ball *toward* the hole was foreign to him.

Standing on the first tee at Disney World, I hunched down and met eyes with Scott, who was decked out in tube socks and an oversized golf shirt.

"Scott, every time you hit the ball, you want to hit for the pin. Your goal should be to make a hole-in-one if you can."

"What's a hole-in-one, Dad?"

"That's when you hit from the tee and knock the ball into the hole in one shot."

"Is it hard?"

"Very hard. Many people go a lifetime without ever making a hole-in-one. But what you want to do is try to hit the ball into the hole every time."

Scott nodded and I stood up, not really sure if he understood my point. He walked to the junior tee, waggled his club just like a pro, and poked a great drive about 10 yards short of the green on the 125-yard hole.

"Nice shot, Scott; way to go! Now don't forget what I told you about trying to hit the ball in the hole."

"Right, Dad."

What Dad Did Right

BY SCOTT ARMSTRONG

I don't remember the first day I played golf with Dad, but I always loved to hit balls and see them go airborne. What I do remember is that I was never *forced* to play golf. One time, Dad and I drove to a field near an old high school, and he and I started hitting balls. I wasn't into it that day, so Dad let me roam around and do what I wanted to do until he was done. I always felt the freedom to hit balls when I wanted to, not when Dad wanted me to practice. There was no pressure then, and there is no pressure today.

Scott pulled his pitching wedge from his bag, took a few practice swings, then let it fly. The ball bounced twice before rolling into the hole.

Everyone roared their approval, and when I saw a grin sweep across Scott's face after carding his first legitimate birdie, I knew he was hooked on golf. Twenty years later, I can assure you that golf has enriched my relationship with Scott, provided untold hours of enjoyment between us, and helped me teach him important principles about life and God in deeper ways than I'll ever know.

If that's what you want for your children, golf will help because the game has an uncanny ability to teach moral lessons. In addition, golf is a great family game because it provides a superb opportunity for you to spend quality time with your children—time that can be used to teach them about honesty, determination, planning, concentration, and self-encouragement. Here are some additional points:

1. Golf imparts great values. Golf is a sport of integrity and honesty. No black-and-white striped referees walk down the fairways with you. No umpire notices whether you improved your lie or not. You are expected to make the call or ruling, no matter how painful the penalty will be, as pro golfer Tom Kite demonstrated when he once said the ball moved while he lined up an important putt. No one saw the ball move after he apparently touched it with his putter, but Tom called a one-stroke penalty on himself, and it cost him the tournament title and tens of thousands of dollars.

Golf also teaches youngsters respect—for others in your playing group, for the group in front of you, and for the Rules of Golf. You don't see John McEnroe-types wrapping an iron around a tree or digging up a green in frustration. Although everyone has gotten upset and tossed a club toward the bag, temper tantrums should be rare occurrences around the course.

If the kids don't hear you swearing after missing a shot, then they are hearing just the opposite message from the one the world teaches; namely, to go ahead and utter a four-letter word when you blow a shot. Believe me, sooner or later your kids will ask you why you don't swear, thereby opening the door for you to explain why.

2. Golf teaches young players to get along with their elders and their peers. Since players of all ages can comprise a foursome, junior golfers are bound to learn something about standards when they are paired with older players, including their parents or grandparents. Important social skills are imparted on the golf course, skills such as shaking a person's hand upon introduction, addressing elders by "Mr." and "Mrs.", waiting for your turn to hit, marking your ball on the green, and letting faster groups play through.

Let me tell you something about golf as it relates to *your* parents. Golf can bolster your relationship with your father, as it did with mine. You may disagree with your father on your Christian beliefs, your values, and your political views, but when you get together on the golf course, you can put those things aside for a few hours and enjoy being with each other.

You can build on those shared memories together, and perhaps that will lead to an opportunity to share your faith. Maybe it won't, but golf will bring you closer, and God doesn't waste any opportunities.

3. Golf builds character—and reveals character. Character still counts in many quarters, and golf instills important lessons about life. And who best to teach those lessons? You! How you conduct yourself on a golf course is watched and assimilated by your youngsters. They see everything, including your famous "foot wedge" or the way you shave strokes on a long par-5. On the other hand, if they see you sticking with the rules, playing the ball from bad lies, and counting all your strokes while attempting to get your ball out of the bunker, they learn the right lessons about life, and that builds character.

There's something about golf that brings out the best and worst in all of us. If you can remain positive, show good character, and soldier on after notching another "snowman" on your card, your kids will fall into step right behind you.

4. Golf is a great game to have on the résumé. If your children grow up to be decent golfers, a good golf game can open doors in corporate America. A healthy percentage of deal making is struck on the golf course, where relationships are cemented and sales are consummated. Savvy business executives say that they can find out more about a person on a golf course than through any other social activity. Golf has a unique way of unmasking how people handle pressure, as well as displaying their sense of humor, honesty, intensity, concentration powers, and ability to recover. If your adult children can successfully get up and down from a greenside bunker, they can usually handle any "hazard" that comes with their job.

That's what Professor Dan Weilbaker at Northern Illinois University in DeKalb, Illinois, was thinking when he asked his school if he could teach a class called Business Golf 101. A few eyebrows shot up when Professor Weilbaker received permission to teach the course, but then several of his students were hired after playing a round with potential bosses. Students aiming for a degree in sales soon lined up to take his one-day seminar on the do's and don'ts of behavior on the links, which includes the following:

An Expensive Game?

I will not disagree with the assertion that golf can be hazardous to your pocketbook. Country-club memberships can cost tens of thousands of dollars, and monthly fees alone can run more than five hundred dollars per month. The old adage—"If you have to ask how much, you can't afford it"—is definitely true with private clubs.

You may not feel right devoting so much of the family budget to a sport like golf, especially if you have more pressing financial needs on behalf of the Kingdom—a new church building program, paying for the kids' Christian education, or supporting your favorites ministries. Fine. I can totally understand that thinking.

Golf is much like the restaurant industry, however; you can find places to indulge in your pleasure at almost every price range. For instance, you can choose to take the family to an expensive restaurant with snooty maître d's, white linens, and *veau emincée*, but do you have to spend $150 every time you take the family out to eat? No, of course not, since those outings are reserved for special occasions. The rest of the time, you and the family gravitate toward Spaghetti Factory and Chili's restaurants, where the final bill promises to be more modest. When you're looking to eat on the cheap, you clip Taco Bell two-for-one chalupa coupons.

The same mind-set applies to golf. Golf doesn't *have* to be played at the tony country club. With a little resourcefulness, you will find affordable golf at a growing number of semiprivate and municipal courses that discount "off-peak" times (anytime other than Saturdays and Sunday mornings) to attract more business.

Let me tell you another thing that should encourage you. Many pro shops offer deep discounts for junior golf because they want to build the game for the future. What better way to expand the golfing universe than by investing in tomorrow's golfers through discounts today?

These courses often offer ten-dollar "stand-by" rounds to juniors, plus discounts on range balls and lessons. If your town or city has several courses within driving distance, make a few phone calls inquiring about discounts for junior golfers.

If economic circumstances are very tight, here are several more ideas:

- If your son is twelve and up, he can do odd jobs around the pro shop in exchange for free golf. This can mean everything from vacuuming the pro shop and cleaning carts to shagging balls on the practice range.

- Go to the Internet and see whether you can find any deals on Web companies that allow reserve tee times online. Web sites such as www.selecteetimes.com or www.eteetimes.com may have special last-minute rates available.

- Check out twilight rates. Golf in the late afternoon and early evening costs half as much. Conversely, some courses have discounts before 7:00 A.M.

- Driving ranges offer multibucket discount cards. Some even have hourly rates that allow you to hit all the balls you can for a flat fee. (Be thankful you don't live in Tokyo, Japan. Though the Shiba driving range in downtown Tokyo has 155 stalls on three levels, you can expect to wait up to ninety minutes after you've purchased your bucket—at a princely sum, I might add.)

- You can always hit balls for free if you have a bucket of old balls, a ball picker-upper (also known as a shag bag), and an empty football field or and undeveloped parcel of land. Set up buckets at the 50-, 100-, and 150-yard markers and fire away!

- Replace your divots.
- Carry a rake with you into the sand trap.
- Mark your ball on the green.
- Don't drive the golf cart as if you're at the Indy 500.
- And don't talk business—at least for the first six holes.

Weilbaker also counsels students not to rush things. Use the first six holes to learn about the customer's family, hobbies, and background. While playing the middle six holes, try to get a better understanding of the customer's business; then use the final six holes to share ideas about how your business can help with the client's pressing needs. Any deals can be closed at the nineteenth hole—the clubhouse bar and restaurant)—or at a later meeting.

Johnny Miller, an NBC golf analyst and former U.S. Open winner, knows how important golf is in the business world. "Playing golf in business is going to be like being computer-literate. You've got to play golf," he said in a *Golf Digest* magazine article. Johnny's attitude is carried by a growing number of Fortune 500 companies—including IBM, Marriott, and Merrill Lynch—who have sent their junior executives to "business golf" seminars to learn social graces and tactical savvy on the links.

It is important to note that golf is not only for business*men*. Women increase their chances of breaking through the glass ceiling—and winning the respect of men around the company water cooler—if they can play good "business golf" at corporate outings. This fact may help explain why girls and women are taking up golf in unprecedented numbers. The National Golf Foundation says 5.7 million women play golf today, a 24 percent increase over the last decade. What's more, women employed outside the home have ventured onto the golf course twice as much as stay-at-home moms. The Executive Women's Golf Association (check out their Web site at www.ewgnatl.org) is a nonprofit organization that "fosters a spirit of acceptance, dignity, and respect for career-oriented women golfers."

A final note: Business golf also can open the door to sharing your values and your faith with others who wouldn't normally cross your path. Call it "outreach golf."

5. Golf is an international game of the future. The global village is being exposed to golf, and international players from different ethnic and national backgrounds are breathing new life into the game. The best female player in the world is Annika Sorenstam of Sweden. Vijay Singh, a Fijian of Indian ancestry, and Se Ri Pak, a dynamic young woman from South Korea, have captured major titles—the PGA and the U.S. Open, respectively—in recent years. Sergio Garcia of Spain and Shingo Katayama of Japan are exciting, dynamic personalities. International competitions such as the Ryder Cup, the President's Cup, and the Solheim Cup have given the sport a tremendous international platform.

"But I Don't Want to Play Golf"

If your children have never played golf, they may have heard some of the following statements:

1. *"Golf Is Too Boring"*

Compared to rock 'em, sock 'em sports like football and ice hockey, youngsters may find golf as exciting as visiting a great aunt. Actually, golf is a game that keeps you involved from the moment you tee it up. It's you against the course. There are shots to plan, strategies to invoke, disappointments to overcome. Golf is more than hitting the ball and chasing it; the game teaches us how to control our emotions and trust our swings. Boring? No way.

2. *"Golf Is a Sissy Game"*

Golf began as a country-club sport for blue bloods in the Northeast, but that era has gone the way of bowler hats and parasol umbrellas. Golf is an equal-opportunity game, and every city and many small towns have at least one municipal or semiprivate course. Even better, most offer low rates for junior play and a variety of affordable lesson programs. As the popularity of golf experiences a boom in the twenty-first century, golf course construction is trying to keep pace. Municipal and semiprivate courses are opening up at the rate of one per day in the United States, which is sure to present more opportunities for you and the family.

As for being sissy, no one would call Tiger Woods a sissy—at least not to his face. Golfers such as Ernie Els, Davis Love III, David Toms, Justin Leonard, Mike Weir, and Jesper Parnevik are tremendous athletes with excellent hand-eye coordination.

3. *"Golf Takes Too Long to Play"*

This is a problem but not an insurmountable one. Granted, it can take six hours to play a round on a crowded public course, but you don't have to play eighteen holes

---

Bringing Golf to the Kids

Good news: Junior golf is booming. According to the National Golf Foundation, more than 2 million youngsters (ages twelve to seventeen) play golf, and junior programs and junior tournaments have seen double-digit increases in recent years.

Bad news: Golf can be an expensive sport, and there aren't enough public facilities to handle the demand. In large metropolitan areas such as Los Angeles County, there are fewer than twenty-eight public facilities for a population of 5 million, causing the municipal courses to be practically overrun. Whereas a course can only handle 60,000 rounds a year and remain playable, such courses as Griffith Park and Alondra Park average 130,000 rounds annually!

Dozens of cities around the country can't find 150 acres or millions of dollars in their parks-and-recreation budgets to build new courses, and thus they are lagging far behind the demand for golf. A popular Chicago golf guide lists two hundred daily-fee courses in the region, but only eleven lie within the city limits. Fortunately, some steps are being taken by the private sector to make golf more accessible and affordable.

The most notable is the First Tee program, a World Golf Foundation initiative to provide affordable opportunities for children to learn golf and its values. PGA Tour commissioner Tim Finchem has taken a lead role in organizing First Tee, which hopes to have one hundred chapters soon. The idea is to create golf facilities and programs that are affordable to children of all socioeconomic and racial backgrounds. For instance, First Tee is renovating a par-3 course in Columbus, Georgia; funding a junior golf academy in Kentucky; and constructing an indoor training facility in Trenton, New Jersey.

Some PGA pros are taking matters into their own hands. A handful of PGA pros in the Phoenix area—led by Brian Whitcomb—have built a nine-hole course on the "back 40" of the 500 Club Golf Course. The par-30 course is *free* for children eighteen and under during the summer, and then an appropriate fee is charged while the kids are in school. OK, OK, so it's hot in Phoenix, but free golf? Sounds like a great deal to me. Another thing: adults are welcome to play at the nine-hole facility, but they must be accompanied by a junior player. I like that.

Ask around to see what First Tee or junior golf programs (such as "Hook Your Kid on Golf" and "First Swings") are in your area. You'll be glad you did.

---

to have fun. For example, you can play just nine holes. I've gone out on the "back nine" with my sons, Scott and Blake, early in the morning before other golfers made the turn. Executive courses with par-3 holes and a couple of par-4s can be played in two to three hours. Parents of young golfers aged ten and under can play some of the new eighteen-hole "putting courses" springing up around the country.

Even if you have only a few hours after Sunday church, you should still be able to play a par-3 course or at least spend some time at the driving range.

4. "Golf Is a Restrictive Game with Complicated Rules"

Au contraire, if you'll pardon my French. Golf is a sport in which rules and etiquette are woven into the tapestry of the game, but I feel that the rules are a help not a hindrance. I remember Arnold Palmer once said that rules give you freedom and the better you know them, the better you can use them to your advantage when you play.

Example: One time when I was playing the Western Open in Chicago, I stood on the eighteenth tee, a tough finishing hole. Rains had swollen a creek running in front of the green, which resulted in an overflow of "casual water" filling a wooded area to the right of the fairway.

I knew the rules allowed me a free drop on the edge of the fairway if I hit to the right into the overflowing water. I also knew that hitting left would send the ball into a nasty out-of-bounds area. I took out my driver and faded the ball into the casual water, while my playing partner, unaware of the casual water rule, took a mighty whack and hooked the ball left—and out of bounds. Two-shot penalty.

When we walked up the fairway, I found my ball and dropped it at the edge of the fairway with a clear shot to the green.

"Wait a minute," said my playing partner. "You can't do that."

"Yes, I can," I said. "I know the rules."

I got my par.

There's a lot more to know about the rules, which we'll discuss in chapter 8. Meanwhile, let's turn our attention to getting your children started playing this wonderful game.

2

TAKING THEIR TEMPERATURE

Taking up golf can be a daunting prospect for anyone—especially those with little experience in the game—but it doesn't have to be. Children, generally, have no fear when it comes to trying something new. Jesus recognized this when he was descended upon by curious children. When his disciples shooed them away, Jesus said, "Leave the children alone, and don't try to keep them from coming to Me, because the kingdom of heaven is made up of people like this" (Matt. 19:14 HCSB). When it comes to golf, the important thing is that children experience some degree of success when they strike the ball.

How do you know whether your children are interested in trying out the game? It's much like taking their temperature, and you do that by proposing to take them to a driving range. If they are very young, you can hand them a set of plastic clubs and let them beat a whiffle ball around the backyard. Some children will be hot to play, some will be lukewarm, and some will have zero interest, which is fine. The worst thing you can do is pull your children out of tennis lessons or their junior hockey league "because you're going to become a golfer!"

Your approach and attitude say everything to your children. If you command your ten-year-old son with these words: "This summer you're going to take lessons and learn how to play golf," he will believe that he is being "forced" to play the game. He's probably not going to like it.

Instead, *offer* your children the chance to play. Say something like, "Megan, I'm going over to the driving range to hit a few balls. Want to join me? Then we'll go over to Dairy Queen when we're done." Even if Megan only tries to hit ten balls before discovering that the nearby brook is more exciting to explore, she's still associating the word *fun* with golf.

Obviously, if your children *ask* you to take them out to the driving range, that's a pretty good indication that they want to try the game. Many kids, of course, are not that direct with their parents, so you have to watch for clues. If you're watching a few holes of a golf tournament on TV some Sunday afternoon, do any of your children watch with you? (I know, some kids would watch test patterns if that was the only thing on TV, which some pundits have likened to watching golf.)

Another indicator of interest is when kids enjoy viewing golf instructional videos. I can't tell you the number of parents who have come up to me and said that their kids wore out *Power Drives for Kids,* the video Blake and I made to demonstrate how golf can be cool and fun. (As you know, *Power Drives for Kids* is part of the DVD included with this book.) Kids have responded to that video in ways I never imagined possible. One father told me that if Michael Jordan, Tiger Woods, and Blake were lined up shoulder to shoulder and his five-year-old son could choose whom he wanted to spend the day with, he would choose Blake. That's the power of the medium.

Print is another powerful medium. Have you ever spied one of your children thumbing through a golf magazine—at home or at the newsstand? Do your children have any buddies who play golf? If so, have they talked about trying to play the game? Have they asked you to take them out to watch Tiger or Annika the next time a PGA or LPGA golf tournament rolls into town?

You also need to keep your child's temperament and personality in mind. As you know, every child comes into this world with a different God-given personality; I know that has been true with my two sons. Scott is a self-starter who relished hitting four or five hundred practice balls because *he wanted to.* He was content to stay out half the afternoon on the range, even in Florida's sweltering summer heat, setting ball after ball on the practice tee.

Blake, on the other hand, is a social creature who loves having people around him. He can't hit more than a half-dozen balls without chatting up other golfers or walking to the clubhouse to get a drink. I found that it's always better to have Blake invite one of his friends to come along when we practice or play eighteen holes.

A Note from Mrs. VanderGolf

Before you take your youngsters to a nearby golf course or driving range, you should teach them a few things about golf etiquette, or what type of behavior is expected.

There is usually no minimum age for children to putt on a practice green or hit from the driving range, but many courses do not allow children seven and under to play, although these children are usually allowed to ride along in the cart.

Your best bet is to go where kids are welcome—municipal and par-3 courses. Private and semiprivate clubs must be responsive to members, and the dues-paying clientele (usually older, more affluent) are not, shall we say, very tolerant of kids running wild around the grounds.

Golf etiquette must be taught from the earliest years. It can be summed up for young golfers in this way:

- No loud talking.
- No roughhousing.
- No acting out.

In a sense, golf etiquette is the same etiquette that you teach your children for how they should behave Sunday mornings at church. Golf courses are not places for unruly behavior.

Dress is important. Children don't have to wear trendy golf fashions, but a collared polo shirt and decent-length shorts that match are always appreciated. Sagging shorts are definitely not in, nor are any "gang colors." T-shirts are fine at driving ranges but *verboten* at clubs. If your children show up at a club dressed in T-shirts or jeans, they will be asked to leave or buy new shirts and shorts in the pro shop before playing. Being "kicked out" creates a nasty scene that leaves everyone with a bad impression about golf.

As for shoes, your children don't need golf shoes, but leave the black Nike Air Fundamentals at home. Outfit your kids with white sneakers.

If you think all these dress rules and etiquette are a turnoff, remember that it cuts both ways. How would *you* feel if you were practicing your putting and several five-year-old kids kept running in front of your line? How would *you* feel if you were hitting balls on the driving range while two children were fighting over who can hit? How would *you* feel if you were dressed smartly for a round of golf but the kids were outfitted in faded T-shirts and shorts that sagged to their ankles?

I'll go over everything you'll want to know about golf etiquette in chapter 7.

The best way to interest your kids in golf is to pile everyone into the car and drive to a nearby driving range and let them putt around on the practice green. Putting is the least intimidating part of golf, and I especially recommend this approach for moms. After your kids putt a few times, they'll tell you in words or in body language if they're having a good time. I'm betting they'll want to do it again!

The First Time Out

You don't have to wait for your kids to give you hints that they want to play golf. Many parents expose their children to the game by just having them tag along when they go to the driving range, which is just fine. Knowing that, what is an optimum age to have your children start swinging clubs?

Any age under ten is ideal because in the primary school years, kids are soaking up knowledge and new stuff rather effortlessly. I say the younger the better because nearly every kid gravitates to a sport involving a stick and a ball. How young is too young? Probably under three years of age. I know Tiger Woods was swinging a club before he could walk, but three years of age is about right for toddlers to attack plastic balls in the backyard with their plastic clubs. Arnold Palmer, one of the great golfing personalities of this past century, said his father made a special set of golf clubs for him when he was three years old. "I was lucky," said Arnie. "I learned to hold a club the right way when I was young, so the proper grip has always been second nature to me."

Three years of age is no magic number. I've always believed that kids have to be in kindergarten or first grade before they can make a good swing with a cut-down or junior club. The primary school years are an excellent time to expose your kids to the game. If they are keen on competition, they must start before age twelve if they are to gain any traction in junior golf.

One of the best grassroots efforts to expose young children to golf is an initiative spearheaded by the National School Golf Program (NSGP). Pilot learn-to-play-golf programs are underway in more than 140 elementary schools involving 65,000 students. The NSGP was by an organization called Golf 20/20.

"The fit of golf and physical education programs is perfect," said Dr. George Graham of the Department of Kinesiology at Penn State University, who is a consultant for Golf 20/20. "It's what teachers are looking for. Golf is a sport of a lifetime, equally appealing to boys and girls. The game is good physical exercise and emphasizes positive character values. Body size is not a factor."

The NSGP not only equips children with the skills of golf, but also it uses the game to teach nine essential character values: honesty, integrity, respect, confidence, responsibility, courtesy, sportsmanship, perseverance, and judgment. The NSGP uses the equipment and coaching system developed by SNAG, which is a modified golf game using plastic clubs and soft tennislike balls to ensure both a safe and fun experience for the students. This program is headquartered in Ponte Vedra Beach, Florida, and is available through their Web site, www.nationalschoolgolf.com. For information on SNAG, go to www.snaggolf.com.

Generally speaking, you want to interest children in golf *before* their teen years because kids usually set themselves down certain sporting paths after they turn thirteen or fourteen. As kids leave middle school for high school, they must declare which sports they will pursue because to make the team at the high school level, they need experience and ability.

Some Yardage Markers

I'll describe how you can help your kids properly grip a club and make a sound, fundamental swing in the next chapter, but for now, let me give you some ideas for introducing golf to your youngsters at various ages.

Three to Six Years Old

If your children are preschoolers, buy some plastic clubs and balls and let them hack away in the backyard. I recommend purchasing oversized whiffle balls or colored foam balls that are heavy enough for kids to "feel" the hit of the ball. When small children successfully strike these oversized balls, they build confidence.

Gillian Bannon, a golf teaching professional in Auckland, New Zealand, is the Pied Piper of golf in the South Pacific. In working with preschoolers, she has found that those who hit golf balls first and then oversized balls experience far less success than preschoolers who start with the oversized balls. "Interestingly, if students were a little apprehensive about golf, I started them with hitting the larger balls, which won them over and assured success the first time they went to hit a golf ball," she told me.

With preschoolers, you can use *really* oversized substitutes, says Gillian. She often starts kids with brooms and lets them whale away at beach balls, vinyl footballs, and small pillows.

The Risk of Burnout

If you're a golf nut—or a parent who thinks golf is the sure-ticket avenue to a college scholarship or a pro career—then you'll have to watch how hard you push your children. Yes, we often have to prod our children (otherwise how do they ever get anything done?), but golf should be seen as one component of a well-rounded childhood. If your kids hear you talking about golf and nothing else, they'll figure that golf is more important to you than your faith. If your kids see you putting on the living room carpet every chance you get instead of cracking open a Bible, they'll know what's really important to you. You need to keep some balance in *all* aspects of your life—spiritual, mental, and physical.

I've seen dozens of kids burn out over the years, and it didn't happen because they played too much but because Dad and Mom took the fun out of the game and put the pressure on. When kids start playing at a young age, their attention span may hold for two holes. If this is the case, don't force them to stay out there longer.

Another way that golfing fathers ensure their children grow up disliking golf is having their nonplaying kids accompany them for eighteen holes. Walking a five-hour round can feel like a death march; riding in a cart can be just plain boring. Think about it: if you sat in a cart for four to six hours doing nothing, wouldn't you be bored out of your skull and hate golf? Yet, that is what some parents do.

When Blake rode in a cart with me, I made sure he had other things to do, like getting an ice cream from the "drink cart," playing a hand-held video game, or reading a magazine. I closely regarded his attention span. On more than a few occasions, we went in before the round was finished.

Remember: Kids want to *do* things, and sitting in a golf cart while Dad walks into a hazard to find his ball, or asks friends for yardage counts, and/or takes his sweet time lining up putts is definitely *b-o-r-i-n-g.* Nope, when you take your kids to the golf course, make sure it's to play with *them.* I can't tell you how many times I took Blake out in the cart with me, supposedly to play with him, yet I got caught up in my own game. I wish I hadn't done that.

There's another thing that Gillian does in her clinics. She takes a photo of each youngster as they are putting or making a drive, and then she gives that photo to the child. The picture implants in the child's mind that he or she is a "golfer."

Seven to Ten Years Old

For older youngsters who have never played the game, let them hit oversized balls with junior-sized clubs in the backyard or in a nearby field. At this age, they are ready to putt and enjoy rolling the ball into the cup. They are also old enough to start hitting "real" shots.

Ten to Twelve Years Old

Preteens who have never played can pass "Go" and head right for the driving range. Start them on the putting green, but don't be surprised if they are itching to try their hand at hitting range balls.

Thirteen to Eighteen Years Old

It's not too late for teens to play golf for the first time. Progress happens rapidly at this age because their bodies are nearing maturity, and they learn quickly. After some rudimentary instruction from you, stand back and let them practice as much as they want. It's important that they begin hitting with the short irons—the 7-, 8-, and 9-irons—because these are the easiest clubs to loft the ball into the air. If they experience rapid success, take them out on a par-3 course.

Golf is a confidence-builder for sons and daughters who are not the swiftest, tallest, or most coordinated in their classes. Nor is golf a team sport in which they are picked last or exiled to right field or the bench. Golf can be played and practiced alone, although it's more sociable to play with others. Every child will find his or her niche in this sport that has plenty of room for all comers.

Finding the Right Clubs

Several golf club manufacturers are producing clubs just for kids, and these are worth checking out. Not only are these clubs the right lengths; they also have the correct weight and flex. Paul Herber, president of TaylorMade, developed a sophisticated fitting system after measuring hundreds of school kids in the San Diego area. Charting the kids' swing speeds helped in the design of the shaft.

Here are some junior club manufacturers worth checking out. And remember, discount golf shops and warehouse clubs often sell for a cheaper price.

La Jolla Club

The Set: They sell a Snoopy set for kids approximately three to five years old; a Blue set for kids approximately six to eight years old; a Yellow set for youngsters approximately nine to eleven years old; and a Green set for those approximately eleven and up.

The Cost: At this writing, the Snoopy set is $59; the Blue set is $159; the Yellow set is $159; and the Green set is $159.

Selling Point: La Jolla Club is a leader in junior clubs. Sets come in three lengths with Super Flex Graphite shafts on oversize heads. They are also available in steel for kids with swing speeds more than 65 mph. Their fitting system is designed to fit by size, not age.

For More Info: Call (800) 468-7700, or visit their Web site at www.lajolla club.com.

U.S. Kids Golf

The Set: The Red set is for kids approximately three to five years old; the Blue set is for kids approximately six to eight years old; the Green set is for kids approximately nine to eleven years old; and the Gold set is for kids approximately eleven and up. Individual clubs are also available.

The Cost: Starter sets can cost from $99 to $169.

Selling Point: These are lightweight, high-flex clubs for beginners in all age groups.

For More Info: Call (888) 3-USKIDS, or visit their Web site at www.uskids golf.com.

Taylor Made

The Set: The 320K junior sets come with one wood, three irons, a putter, and a stand bag and in three models designed to fit kids of different ages and sizes (K-30, K-40, and K-50).

The Cost: $250

Selling Point: Each club has an elongated handle; for example, one club is a 5- or 6-iron depending on where it's gripped. The Growth Guarantee program allows outgrown clubs to be replaced for a $100 fee.

For More Info: Call (800) TAYLORM (829-5676), or visit their Web site at www.taylormadegolf.com.

Ping

The Set: Three different Pal Junior packages: Junior Executive, Junior Medalist, and Junior Champion.

The Cost: $210 to $350

Selling Point: Each package contains various irons, woods, putter, and a bag.

For More Info: Call (800) 4-PING-FIT (474-6434), or visit their Web site at www.pinggolf.com.

Remember, your kids don't need a full set of clubs. Charlie Sorrell, one of *Golf* magazine's Top 100 Teachers, won't allow his junior players to have anything more in their bag than a 5-wood, 3-iron, 5-iron, 7-iron, pitching wedge, sand wedge and putter until they break 85!

Once you think you see genuine interest on your child's part, you will have to think about enrolling them in a lesson program. I'll have more to say on professional instruction in chapter 11.

"There can be no natural, free-flowing swing when the mind is involved in instructing the body."
—J. H. TAYLOR

3
=

So They Want
to Get Started

$\boxed{P}$ leeeze, can we go play golf?" says Matt, your second-grader. "Pretty please?"

"Me, too. I wanna golf right now," chips in Kristen, your four-year-old.

Who can resist? Certainly not fathers or mothers who love their kids and would be pleased to see their youngsters become golfers.

The moment of truth has arrived. You've decided to pack the kids in the car and drive off to the driving range or local golf course. In this chapter, I'm going to assume that you—the parent—are not terribly knowledgeable about golf, but as I said earlier, you don't have to be a golf nut to get your kids into golf. Besides, I want to encourage any moms reading this book that you are just as capable as dads of introducing golf to your children. Granted, there is a time and place for professional lessons, but when the kids are just starting, you can create a positive impression and teach them the fundamentals of a good golf swing.

How you teach those fundamentals depends very much on your children's ages and their maturity. You can't explain things to younger kids in the same manner that you speak to teenagers. What works with a seven-year-old may sound silly to a seventeen-year-old. Before you actually start hitting balls, however, you must present a few guidelines to your kids, no matter what their age. Take them aside and say:

- "Always check behind you before you swing. If you accidentally hit someone with your club, you could really hurt that person."
- "Never hit a golf ball at somebody. Always hit straight ahead into the open field."
- "Take care of your equipment. That means not hitting stones or concrete. Golf clubs are only used on grass or in sand bunkers."

Getting Started

How to swing a golf club has been the subject of thousands of books and magazine articles, but much to my dismay, the instruction has been long on technique and short on practicality. We golf pros have made the swing way too complicated for the average beginner.

Case in point. I was teaching a parent/child golf clinic outside Seattle when I asked a cute three-year-old to step forward and hit a ball in front of the entire audience. I had seen him hitting the ball well earlier, so I knew he was a natural. The boy didn't fail me; he stepped up to the ball and knocked it forty yards straight ahead, easy as apple pie.

The crowd clapped, and then I asked him to hit another shot. This time when he started his backswing, I grabbed his club so he couldn't swing.

"Peter, I want you to look at me."

I could tell Peter was wondering why I stopped him in the middle of his backswing.

"Peter, I want you to listen very carefully and do everything I tell you to do. Understand?"

Peter didn't say anything, but he nodded affirmatively.

"Now Peter, I want you to start all over again, but this time I want you to check your arms first. Make a V with your arms before initiating the backswing. When you start your swing, keep your head down, your left arm straight, and your knees bent. Then turn your shoulders ninety degrees and your hips forty-five degrees, but keep pressure on the inside of your front foot. When you start to bring the club through, make sure you drop your elbow and keep it in your pocket. Oh, and don't forget to pronate your wrists at impact. Got it?"

No, he didn't have it. Kids—and parents—do not learn by a detailed break-down of the stroke mechanics; they learn by imitating what they see. All the explaining in the world won't be as effective as watching someone make a good swing and then imitating it.

When my son Scott was in a stroller, he used to watch me hit practice balls by the hour, and one day he started imitating my swing. Sitting in his stroller, he took his plastic club and brought it back left-handed because that was a mirror image of my right-handed swing. When he graduated to hitting plastic balls in the back-yard, he insisted on whacking the ball left-handed, no matter how much I tried to get him to turn him around and hit right-handed. I didn't want him to be a lefty because left-handed clubs are hard to find, and I knew his right hand was dominant. Scott persisted, however, and I relented. He hits left-handed today, though he writes and eats with his right hand. What this story illustrates is how strong the power of imitation can be—which, by the way, is an important spiritual lesson as well, isn't it?

Many parents have come up to me after one of my clinics and said, "But Wally, I haven't golfed much. What if I don't have a good swing to imitate?"

If asking a family friend to demonstrate a good swing is not practical, I'm confident you can get your children started anyway. The power of suggestion and your enthusiasm are

---

A Different Type of Training Aid

If your children are young—ten years old or younger—they will listen to an analogy that says the Bible can be looked upon as a training aid for our lives. That's why it's important to read the Bible and become familiar with it so that we can apply it to our lives. Jeremiah 30 talks about listening to the voice of the teacher, very much like how we should listen to the voice of a golf pro.

When we practice, we must listen to that voice and remember what he said about improving our swing. In the same way, if we go through life listening to God's voice that we heard in the Bible, it can only improve our lives and the decisions we make.

strong forces of encouragement, and if you convey to your children you're *sure* they will learn a good swing, they will learn it.

Let me encourage you one step further. Inside every person and every child is a golf swing. I'll help you learn how to draw out that swing through training aids, imitation, and analogies to other sports. Much of what I cover in this chapter and the next two chapters can also be found on the *First Tee Shot* DVD. Be sure to check it out too.

Starting the Swing Movement

I've listened to my share of negative instruction about the swing over the years, and it's based on the assumption that performing the golf swing correctly is an unnatural movement. This attitude dates back to the turn of the century, when the golf swing was taught like a Rube Goldberg-like series of pulleys and levers that had the arms and legs going every which way. Writers of that era said that golf was about as natural as getting in a car and attempting to drive with the steering wheel stuck in the passenger's door.

Ben Hogan, one of the great players of the 1940s and 1950s, made the following statement: "If one tends to play the game by natural instinct, he would never finish a round." Percy Boomer, a contemporary of Hogan who wrote several influential golf instructional books, said, "Often, the natural, soundest, and permanently profitable motion in the golf swing feels unnatural." (Try saying that seven times in a row.)

Ben Hogan also said that the swing, which takes one to two seconds to complete, produces "twenty-nine different body movements" that the golfer must track. That may be true, but can the conscious mind give twenty-nine commands in that time span and still produce a fluid swing? I don't believe it can.

I teach the golf swing in an entirely different manner, using word pictures, images, and training aids. If you do the drills found in this book with your children, they will be given the means to *feel* the correct swing. Once your children start swinging the club correctly, they can practice it and reinforce the muscle memory needed to produce a good swing time after time. Practice makes permanent.

Getting a Grip

Before we get too far along, we should talk about the grip. A correct grip enables the wrists to load on the backswing and unload on the forward swing. I don't want to get too technical here, but a good grip is the foundation of a good swing.

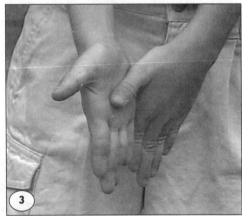

Direct your child to stand up straight, clap his hands, and grab the lower hand's thumb with the top hand (see photos 1 and 2).

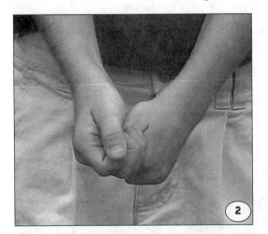

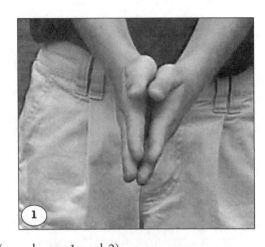

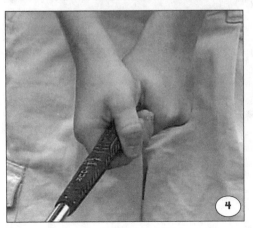

Then open the fingers so that they point to the ground, with the top hand's thumb in the palm of the bottom hand (see photo 3). Now slip a club between your child's fingers and let him put his fingers, then hands, around the grip. Check to see that the lower hand rolls over and rests on the top hand's thumb and that the lower hand's thumb is positioned on the target side of the shaft (see photo 4).

Whew! I know that's a lot of detailed instruction, but now that your child is gripping the club, do a final check:

1. Your child should be able to waggle the club back and forth loosely (see photo 5).
2. The hands should face each other.
3. The club should be between the fingers.
4. The lower hand's thumb should be on the side of the shaft facing the ball.

Be sure after she takes her grip that she can comfortably cock her wrists and lay the club back on her back shoulder.

Last but not least, remind your child to grip firmly but not tightly. Say, "Imagine holding a frog. That's how hard you want to grip the club."

"Oh, Dad, a frog? That's gross!"

The Stance

I'll have more to say about the stance later, but for now, just make sure the knees are slightly bent and the arms are hanging freely. A correct stance provides the base to produce a powerful swing through the ball.

I think that covers the basics. Now your kids are ready to start swinging the club. To do that, you will need a hula hoop to help you teach a good "circle swing."

The Circle Swing

Listen up, Mom and Dad: Your kids can develop a good swing by becoming a good circle maker. Swinging in a circle allows them to hit the ball straight and into the air. Here's what you should say to your children:

"Josh, to play golf, you need a good swing. A good swing is making a circle as you swing. Remember, there is no up and down or chopping motion in the swing. The swing is the most important thing, and if you can make a good swing, you're going to hit a good shot. What you want is to have the ball simply get in the way of a good circle swing."

The best way for your child to see, feel, and understand his own circle swing is for you to take a hula hoop and hold it over him (see photos). Have him swing in slow motion underneath it, backward and forward, watching where his hands go and how it feels. Put a 9-iron in his hands when he's starting out, not a driver or 3-wood.

35

If possible, have the other parent or another adult take videos of you holding the hula hoop while Josh makes a good circle swing. Make sure Josh stays loose and relaxed in the shoulders and arms. The club should be held firmly but not too tight. After he gets the hang of making a circle swing, check his grip by saying, "Do you have a good grip, Josh? Let's see. Remember to clap your hands and hold them together. Then take the club and grip it, pretending you are holding a frog because you don't want to squeeze too hard. As you swing, the circle will gain power when the club is held firmly but not tightly."

The hula hoop is the most effective training aid you can have. When working with the hula hoop, hold it over your child as shown in the photos. Have the child swing underneath in very slow motion. Be sure to stand far away so he doesn't strike your legs with the club. Tell him to watch his hands and how the clubhead makes a circle as he swings.

More Props

I'm not the only golf pro with a bag of props. Charlie Sorrell, a good friend of mine who owns the Golf Meadows teaching facility south of Atlanta, not only uses a hula hoop, but he also uses milk jugs, carpet rolls, and water wings to help teach golf to kids.

One of his best teaching aids involves taking two six-by-six-inch pieces of wood, maybe four feet long. He then has the child stand on one of these balance beams and hit a ball that is resting on the other beam. "This exercise teaches them balance," says Charlie.

He also has come up with dozens of rhymes that he incorporates into his lessons—catchy sayings that stick in the minds of youngsters. Sure, they're a little corny, but kids won't forget them:

- "The more up and down you go, the more you'll enjoy the show."
- "The player who swings and falls back . . . will never get the ball on track."
- "Wrists that are tight . . . destroy ball flight!"
- "Wrists that are limber . . . keep you out of the timber."
- "Let the forearms cross . . . show the ball who's boss!"
- "If you're caught squattin' . . . your shot will be rotten."
- "Incline your spine . . . and your swing will be fine."
- "If you swing too much around, you could be out of bounds."

If you'd like more rhymes and solid instruction, they can be found in Charlie's book *Lessons That Rhyme . . . Stay in the Mind*. (Call 770-957-8786 to order.)

The second time you try this, ask him to feel the clubhead going around just underneath the hoop on the backswing and on the way through. Then simply stand back and let him swing through the ball, feeling the circle motion with each swing. This needs to be done over and over until he has a clear picture of the circle swing. Have him watch his hands as he takes the club back, and then ask him to watch the ball as he starts to bring the club forward.

Now that you have your child learning the feel of the circle swing, it's time to introduce the *power circle swing* and the *accurate circle swing,* (sometimes called the *full-power swing* and the *short swing* for accuracy).

The reason for two different-length swings is that there are two different games within the game of golf—the long game and the short game (or long shots and short shots). What's important is that you start your children with short backswings and then progress to the longer power swings. Remember: it is a progression. You didn't teach your children how to run before they could walk, did you?

Have the kids first practice their short backswings by putting or chipping tennis balls or plastic balls in the backyard. (Never let them use golf balls around the house because sooner or later a window will break.) Once they've chipped around the house, take them to a driving range or club and let them chip onto putting greens. They need to develop a feel for distance when they swing.

The *accurate circle swing* is like the pendulum on a grandfather clock—not too much of a backswing, not too much of a follow-through. It would be like taking the club back to 8:00 P.M. and swinging to 4:00 P.M. Or you can say, "Josh, swing like an elephant trunk" as you make a short-swing motion with your dangling arms. The short swing is a ticktock, one-two motion. Do you have a metronome in the house? Play it as your youngsters chip plastic balls in the backyard.

If you have several children learning this short circle swing at the same time, you can play "Simon Says" with them:

- "Simon Says make half a circle."
- "Simon Says make a tiny circle."
- "Touch the ball with your club. Gotcha!"

Once your kids get the hang of the circle (using the hula hoop discussed earlier), they can learn to make the *power circle swing,* which is the Barry Bonds of golf shots. This is the full swing—with a distinct ready, load, and fire sequence—designed to send the ball as far as it will go. We will describe the power circle in full detail in the next chapter.

Once your children have the hang of both swings, here's another game you can play with them:

> "OK, kids, I want you to think about driving a car. You lightly put the foot down and start going ten miles per hour. Give me a circle swing that is going only ten miles an hour. Now increase it to thirty miles an hour. Fifty miles an hour. One hundred miles per hour!"

You can "change speeds" and have them make corresponding swings according to the "miles per hour" they are traveling.

After you've worked with the hula hoop, here are some other analogies that will leave an impression on your children. I've written them as you would talk to your youngster:

- "The golf swing is like a sling shot. The ground and your legs are the handle, and your body and arms are the sling. You want to feel like the golf club is slinging through the air as you hit the ball."
- "For the backswing, pretend you are pitching a football to a tailback. Can you do that for me?"
- "Another way to look at the backswing is by pretending you are sweeping the dust off home plate with a broom."
- "When your backswing goes all the way back, you should feel as though you are holding a waiter's tray at the top of the swing. Can you take a backswing and then stop at the top so we can see if you're holding a waiter's tray?"
- "When you make the forward swing, you want to feel as if you are striding like a baseball batter or pitcher. It's also called shifting your weight from the back foot to the front foot."

- "Another way to look at the swing is to pretend you are kicking a football soccer-style. Plant yourself and hit."

If you are an experienced golfer, show the swing, don't say it. Keep words to a minimum, as I have in these descriptions. Remember to be patient, talk slowly, and stay away from describing the mechanics.

What's Their Learning Style?

All kids don't learn the same. Just as kids have differing temperaments and personalities, they also have particular ways of learning. Three senses through which children absorb and learn new information are visual, auditory, and kinesthetic. Let's look at how these senses apply to learning golf.

If your child is a *visual learner,* then he learns best by watching you (or the pro) make the swing and hit the ball. As I said before, kids are great imitators, and if you demonstrate and show them how it's done, they progress quickly. It won't do anyone any good to explain the swing to visual learners. They'll just get confused.

I've always felt that 85 percent of kids (and adults) are visual learners, which is why I use so many props on the lesson tee. Just show and go!

There will always be a few kids who are *auditory learners.* These youngsters are good listeners and like things explained to them. Auditory learners like to talk about golf and what they are doing. In other words, they are verbal and enjoy people.

Finally, there are the *kinesthetic learners.* These golfers hit by "feel." If they strike a ball well, you should excitedly ask, "Did you feel that one? You did? Great! That's how it's supposed to feel. Here's another ball. Now hit it again."

Determining your children's learning style and adapting your teaching methods to match will help them learn the game—and you'll be able to help them with their homework as well!

Parental Checkpoints

As you're introducing the circle swing to your children, be aware of each child's attention span. With preschoolers, five minutes might be max. Primary school children should be able to hang with you for fifteen minutes.

Give lots of "attaboys" and "attagirls." Keep the fun level high. Those who say that kids don't learn unless they are soberly setting themselves to the task don't know kids. Once you feel your daughter has a solid circle swing, take a blindfold and cover her eyes. Then stand back and see whether she can hit the ball blindfolded. If she does loft the ball into the air, act excited and make a big deal out of it.

I have plenty more drills you can do with your youngsters after they've developed their circle swings. If you think they're ready, turn to the next chapter.

4

SOMETHING BORROWED, SOMETHING NEW

*T*hroughout my years of teaching, I've found that images are much more powerful than words. This shouldn't surprise me since Jesus often spoke in parables, using trees, seeds, and other items to help get his message across. Just as he knew what his audience was capable of understanding, you, too, should make use of props when you're teaching kids; that way, they'll better understand how to swing a golf club. As you'll see, you can use footballs, mops, sponges, PVC pipes, and brooms to accomplish that goal and create excitement.

Kids love surprises, which is why it's important to surprise them with a training aid—something they can see, feel, and swing. (You can see many of these training aids in the *First Tee Shot* DVD.)

Getting Ready

It is so important that you continually check your youngsters' grip. Be sure to go over the key elements discussed in the last chapter and review the DVD often so that the kids understand completely how to place their hands on the club. Three key pressure areas need to be practiced, and you can practice these by simply using a dime. So get a dime and follow along with these drills.

1. In a good grip, the hands need to be connected. Give your son the dime and have him put it on the top of his upper thumb. As he closes his lower hand around it, have him squeeze it down under the lifeline of his back hand. Then have him try

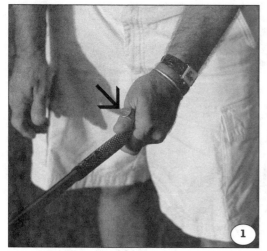

hitting some golf shots by keeping pressure down on top of that thumb throughout his swing. Do not let the dime fall out. (See photos 1 and 2.)

2. Another dime drill is to place a dime under the pad of your daughter's forward hand and squeeze it under the top of her palm. Again, do not let it fall out. Kids have a tendency to let the clubhead slip out of their left hand on the backswing. (See photo 3.)

3. A third dime drill is to put the dime in the crease between the back hand's thumb and forefinger. Take your young golfer's back hand and place it on the club, then put the dime in that crease and have him squeeze it. Play some shots and do not let the dime fall out. If there is a gap between his thumb and forefinger on his back hand, the club will slip up and down as he makes his swing. (See photo 4.)

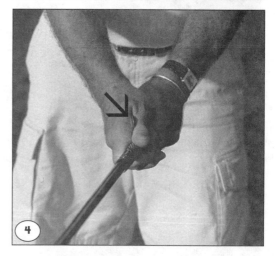

Stance and Alignment Drills

Not only is it important to have your child get into a good, solid athletic stance, but he must also aim the circle and place the ball in the right position in the stance. As the club comes around and contacts the ball, it will be sent in the right direction and with the correct ball-to-club contact. The best way to achieve this is to take the time to build a teaching station to practice in, not only when your child is practicing at home with the training aids but also on the practice tee. Through consistent proper use of this teaching station for practice, your child will memorize the correct mechanical positions of setup and alignment. When he or she goes out on to the golf course, these fundamentals will be automatic—the end result of all practice.

To build a station, simply take two clubs (or you may decide to use two pieces of PVC pipe or two yardsticks), and lay one club down with the grip pointed just to the left of the target. Then place the other club at a ninety-degree angle to the first one. Have the child straddle this club and place a ball a few inches away from its end. As he gets into his stance, check to be sure that his feet, hips, and shoulders line up with the club that is pointing toward the hole.

As the youngster plays different shots, he simply takes his stance in different positions, straddling the club. For irons, the ball should be placed right below his nose. For woods, the ball should be placed just off the tip of his front shoulder. Also for the driver, the ball should be teed up high enough so that the top of the clubhead rests in the middle of the ball.

The Quarterback Drill

This is one of the favorite drills that I use in Scott's instructional tape. Your kids can learn the correct posture, as well as the start of the backswing, by simply playing quarterback for a few minutes.

Take a football out in the backyard or even take it to the practice tee and have your players set up as a quarterback who is taking a snap. You can see the adult golfer in the picture is in this position. Notice that his knees are flexed. He is bent over from the waist, but his back remains straight. His arms are hanging naturally, but his chin is up slightly off his chest. His weight is evenly split between his legs.

From this position, the kids can practice a handoff to a running back, which is just like the start of the golf backswing. The pros call this a one-piece backswing because the body and arms simply twist altogether and allow the club to make a nice circular arch away from the ball.

Swing Circle Practice

Two of my favorite training tools to use in developing the swing circle are a streamer and a tempo ball. These are demonstrated quite extensively in Blake's instructional tape.

Surveyors Tape on a Stick

This colorful tape is available at a hardware store. Use a short piece of PVC pipe for the stick and drill a hole in the end. Attach six to eight feet of tape to the stick and direct your child to make large, sweeping circles slowly above the head and then down into a golf swing—swinging back and forth and back and forth. When he swings through the bottom of the circle, have him pop the tape. It is like cracking a whip.

Then have your child do the same drills with a golf club and ultimately play some shots. This back-and-forth circular repetition will build the feelings of timing and power that he needs.

Tempo Ball

Make your tempo ball with a shoe string, a tennis or whiffle ball, and a dowel. The total length should be about the length of an 8-iron. Tempo balls may also be purchased in manufactured form.

Be sure your child starts the backswing by winding up the shoulders and the forward swing by shifting the weight forward. Be sure the ball swings back, and

through, touching him just below the shoulder and above the elbow line on each side. Check that he doesn't start winding back, or unwinding forward, until the ball taps his body. The key to a good swing is good tempo, not swinging hard.

To help your child understand where the power comes within the circle, you may wish to use the following two tools. These are found within the *First Tee Shot* DVD.

1. Power Broom. This drill will teach your child the correct backswing and the setting of the wrists, which is essential for building up power and releasing it through the swing. Start by taking a household broom and cutting the handle to the length of a 5-iron. Paint one side of the broom's bristle end green and the other side red (or any duo of other bright colors). Also paint one corner white, as you can see in the photo above.

As your child practices, be sure that on the backswing he sweeps the broom so that one color is halfway back and at the top. Then as he comes forward, he will change the colors as he goes through impact, swishing the broom. Tell him that he wants to feel like he is changing the colors of the clubhead as he makes his backswing and forward swing. This is a surefire way to promote a fluid releasing action of the hands, arms, and club through the hitting area. The broom will also build muscles!

2. Toe Up to Toe Up Drill. Put a peel-off label on the face and back of the club and draw a toe or an arrow on it. Have your young golfer watch the toe or arrow up when her hands are swinging waist high on each side of her swing (see photos 1 and 2).

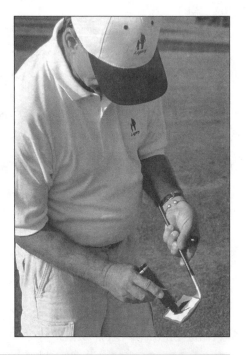

The toe or arrow should point toward the target at the top of the swing (see photo 3). The wonderful thing about using the stickers is that your child can hit balls with the tape on the face, enabling him or her to see and feel the correct positions.

The great thing about all of the practice-training tools that I have demonstrated is they can be used not only on the practice tee but also in your backyard or in a park using tennis balls. Always have the child practice four or five times with the training aid and then take the club and play four or five shots with a golf ball or tennis ball. That way the child will begin to develop and memorize the correct swing fundamentals necessary to become a great circle maker.

Lastly, kids love to do these exercises with the parents. Make up an extra tempo ball streamer and stickers and have at it right along with the kids! You just might improve your own golf game in the meantime.

5

GETTING DRILLED

B lake was nine years old when we filmed *Power Drives for Kids,* but unlike Scott, Blake had never been a range rat content to beat balls under a blazing sun.

The fact that Blake hadn't really gotten into golf was fine with me, and I wanted to practice what I preached. If Blake wanted to play ice hockey, which he did, I wasn't about to flap my arms and tell him he couldn't do that. Thus, on the infrequent occasions when we went golfing, I made sure we had tons of fun, followed by an ice cream treat.

The *Power Drives* video shoot was scheduled at the TPC at Avenel Club in Potomac, Maryland. While the camera crew was setting up, I thought it would be a good idea to have Blake shake the cobwebs out of his swing. Since Blake was a fourth grader who hadn't played much golf, I figured a few butterflies were ruffling around his stomach.

"Let's see how you're hitting them," I coached.

Blake gripped the club and went through his usual preshot routine. Then he drew back his club, started the downward swing, and whiffed the ball!

The poor boy's nervous, I thought.

"That's OK, Blake," I offered. "The ball is still waiting for you to hit it," I said, trying to bring a little levity to the moment.

Blake drew back his club a second time, started the downward swing, and whiffed the ball again. *How are we going to film a video if Blake can't hit the ball?* I thought.

From my trained eye, I knew Blake didn't have much of a swing. For a fleeting moment, I thought we would be filming the world's greatest demonstration of an evolving golf swing. At this point, all I wanted was a couple of decent shots from Blake.

"Try again."

Blake had the ball teed up too high, but I figured that was the least of his problems. His third, fourth, and fifth swings made contact—if you can call topping the ball in the direction of the women's tees good contact.

Time out!

We had brought a dozen training aids to the video shoot, so I picked up a two-foot-high baseball tee used for T-ball. I placed a golf ball on the tee and handed Blake a baseball bat. "Hit that," I said.

Blake got into a batting stance that imitated his favorite baseball player—Sammy Sosa of the Chicago Cubs. He stepped up to the ball and pretended he was standing at home plate inside the friendly confines of Wrigley Park. Then he stepped into the ball and smacked it with all his might.

"Great, Blake. Try it again."

He crushed that ball and the next one too.

Then I took the high tee away and gave him back his golf club. "Show me how Sammy Sosa would hit a golf ball."

Blake did the most awesome thing. He lifted up his front foot and strode into the shot, creaming the ball about 150 years down the fairway, straight as an arrow.

And that is how our baseball drill evolved, which I'll be telling you about in this chapter, along with several other drills. What Blake's story says is that he was trying too hard to hit the golf ball instead of relying on his body to make the shot. What I had to do was take his mind off how to hit the ball and replace it with a fun drill that he could *imitate.*

Keep this point in mind as you experience frustrating outings when your kids whiff the ball or top it ten yards. Hitting a golf ball is much more difficult than we bargain for. You may be thinking, *The ball is just sitting up on a tee, waiting to be hit,* but that stationery ball can be extremely difficult to strike well.

What Equipment Should They Have?

Sir Winston Churchill, the British prime minister during World War II, once said this about one of his favorite sporting pastimes: "Golf is a game whose aim is to hit a very small ball into an even smaller hole with weapons singularly ill-designed for the purpose."

I think of that quotation when parents ask me what golf equipment their children should have. I find no reason to start beginning golfers with a new bag of clubs. My good friend and longtime pro Bobby McIver recommends that parents of small children (eight and under) take an old high-lofted club like a 7-wood, have it cut down by their local pro, and let the children flail away at a tennis ball. "Small children should be able to get it airborne with a 7-wood, which will keep them coming back for more," Bobby said in an interview.

One thing to avoid, however, is giving your kids a complete set of cut-down clubs because they could be too heavy to swing properly. Heavy clubs and big, fat grips prevent your children from learning a good circle swing, forcing them to lift and chop the club. When they start hitting at the driving range and chipping around the green, make sure your kids are playing with junior clubs that are properly weighted for them.

Hand-me-downs or a decent junior set can be purchased at a garage sale or secondhand store (like Play It Again Sports). Generally speaking, youngsters ten and under need a 3-wood, 5-wood, pitching wedge, sand wedge, a handful of irons, and a putter. A 5-, 7-, and 9-iron should be sufficient.

Golf courses—from the haughtiest private reserve to Billy Bob's Range and Par-3 Holer—are fairly adamant about one rule: you must have your own set of clubs when you play. You can't tell the starter that Josh or Missy will "play out of my bag."

There is no reason to purchase a new set of clubs since you don't know whether your children will catch the golf bug, so if your child is eight years old and trying the game, I would borrow clubs from a friend or rent from a pro shop.

The kids won't need golf shoes; for now, they can get away with sneakers. Fortunately, the shoe craze hasn't struck golf as it has in basketball. Nike tried to create an aura with the introduction of Tiger Woods shoes (at two hundred dollars a pair!), but the stylish black and red-trimmed model was targeted for the teen crowd. Big mistake. Parents weren't gullible enough to lay out two C-notes for fashion, which doomed the expensive shoe to the discount table.

Good golf shoes can usually be found on sale for twenty-five to forty dollars. Remember that very few courses allow spiked shoes, so you will have to remove the spikes and replace them with plastic ones.

Many parents (and kids) believe they are resigned to spending many boring hours on the driving range, but it doesn't have to be that way. I've come up with fun drills—using everyday household things like brooms, hula hoops, and Styrofoam cups—that make practicing a blast. When kids perform these drills, they will never notice that they are really practicing *how* to hit a golf ball.

Try the following drills the next time you're on a driving range with your kids.

Cup Crush Drill

This tip is one of my favorites. Tee up a ball and put a Styrofoam cup over it. The ball should be completely under the cup. Next, have your child address the cup and imagine the ball under it. Then give the signal and let him blast the ball out of the cup. Believe it or

not, the ball will shoot down the fairway like a normal shot.

As in karate—where you power through a board instead of chopping at it—your children need to swing through the cup as if nothing is there. This drill will teach them to swing through the ball and hit it further.

Knee Drill

Have your daughter kneel on one knee or both. From this position, ask her to take a circular swing back and through the ball. Let her try to keep the choppiness out of her swing. When she hits the ball, both of you will be surprised how far she can hit it!

Sweepback Drill

This drill will prevent lifting the club at the start of the backswing and will help your child develop the feeling of a smooth, low takeaway and circular arc to the top of the backswing. This also helps promote winding up the shoulders and proper wrist cock at the top.

Place a second ball four to five inches behind a teed-up ball. Have your child brush back the second ball during the backswing. Then play some shots.

Tips for Using the Drills and Training Aids

- When you demonstrate a swing or a drill, show the movement *before* you tell how to do it. Kids will watch what you're doing and not hear what you're saying if you talk as you demonstrate.
- Have your kids practice doing the training aids with their eyes closed. This helps them focus on the feeling of the motion, which will help them feel the swing.
- Ask questions as your children try the swing, such as "Did that feel good?" and "What are you feeling?"
- Use different props because most kids relate differently to each prop.
- If you can show it instead of saying it, you'll be more effective.

Right Foot Back Drill

This drill helps promote an inside-out swing that is common to all great golfers. Have your child take his or her normal address stance. Pull the trail foot back toward the heel of the front foot. Swing from this position and feel the circular arc. Watch Blake illustrate this drill and stop the videotape at the top of his backswing. Be sure your child feels his shoulders and wrists winding up and loading.

Baseball Drill

Have your child address a ball, swing back, and get into her favorite baseball player's stance. Your child will instinctively wind up the shoul-

ders and cock the wrists while doing this drill. Then have her play shots. Be sure the club brushes the ground on the backswing and isn't picked up as in chopping wood. The wrists should cock at the very last minute, at the top of the backswing. I have found this to be the most effective drill on the video. Use this again and again to develop the feeling needed for a powerful golf swing.

Split Grip Drill

This drill will help develop a feel for the correct hinging of the wrists at the top of the backswing and will help the club stay low on the backswing.

Guide your child to address the ball and drop the trail hand down, spreading the hands apart three to four inches. Have your child feel the hands coming through the ball in the correct position, with the right hand crossing over the top of the left to the proper finish position. Practice this drill without a ball first, then hit some balls. Swing in a slow motion first and build to full speed.

Water Balloon Drill

A great way to develop through the ball is to take a water balloon and put it behind a golf ball. Swing through the water balloon and drive the ball out to the fairway. This develops concentration, a good windup, and a solid crack of the club through the balloon.

6

JUST LIKE MIKE

Every spring and summer, Michael Jordan, John Elway, Wayne Gretzky, and a host of other well-known athletes fan out and participate in a variety of celebrity golf tournaments around the country. I love watching six-foot, six-inch Michael Jordan hunching over a four-foot sidehill par-saving putt on the eighteenth hole before thousands in the gallery and a national TV audience. Nobody is protecting the cup, and there are no teammates he can pass the putt to. I imagine his knees are shaking like he's in a Game 7 play-off game.

I have found many parallels between golf and the major sports, and you can use your children's knowledge of basketball, baseball, football, and soccer to teach them about the game of golf. For instance, shooting free throws is very much like hitting a golf shot. No, the golf swing is nothing like the actions of the arms shooting the basketball, but the *preparation* for each free throw is similar to the preparation youngsters must go through before they take the club back and swing away.

I call them "rituals," and every sport has them. In basketball, the free throw ritual is this: the referee hands you the ball, and you place it between your hands and dribble a couple of times. You adjust your stance, get comfortable, and line up with the target—the basket. Your eyes zero in on the rim, and you mentally prepare for the ball to fly through, hitting nothing but net. You bounce the ball two more times, set yourself, and then let the ball fly. *Swish!*

Consider the preshot routine in golf. The tee box is the free throw area. You have to hit behind an imaginary line between the two markers that start each hole. When you walk up to the tee, you initiate a set of rituals: using the left hand to place the ball on the wooden tee, you step back and grip the club, looking at where you want to hit. Then you take a couple of practice swings. When you're ready, you step closer to the ball, setting the clubhead right behind it. You waggle the club several times, perhaps bringing a swing thought to mind. Keeping your eye on the ball, you draw the club back and swing away.

In each sport, you trust what you have practiced. Michael Jordan played basketball seriously for twenty-five years, probably practicing and playing in games 250 days a year. If you figure that he shot 100 free throws each day he played, then Michael aimed 625,000 free throws at the rim during his basketball career. Does MJ have a preshot routine when he steps to the free throw line? Of course. Has he practiced that routine? Yes—over and over and over, a half-million times.

When we become followers of Christ, we're reminded about the importance of spending time with God each day. We develop spiritual muscles by reading God's Word, developing a regular prayer life, and listening to others talk about their walk with Christ. Since our faith grows and matures the more we practice it, it stands to reason that consistent Bible study is the way to "get better" with God.

The same idea holds true in golf. The key is to plan your practice and practice your plan. Then you will understand why the great golfer Ben Hogan once said, "The more I practice,

Forming Good Habits

Let me give you a word picture as you teach your children the basics of golf. Each time your children swing the club, they are forming tiny cobwebs of muscle memory. As they swing the club more and more, those cobwebs will ultimately become a violin string in their elementary school years, and by the time they are teenagers, steel cables over the Golden Gate Bridge.

That's why it's so important for them to learn to swing *correctly* in a circular motion. Habits—good or bad—are hard to break, and if you can help them develop a solid swing in their "cobweb" stage, their swing will strengthen into cables that won't snap under pressure.

This concept is also why Sunday school classes and Christian schools have kids memorize Bible verse after Bible verse when they're young. Talk about muscle memory. Having God's Word form cobwebs of spiritual memory will help our youngsters grow up to be spiritually strong young adults able to withstand the winds of worldly pressure.

the luckier I am on the golf course." Remind your youngsters that golf has goals just like other sports, and golf's goal is to put the ball into the cup. "Holing out" in the fewest number of strokes possible requires practice. In my clinics, I ask kids, "Why do you go to practice soccer all week long if your game's on Saturday?" They know the answer because practice counts.

I talk about soccer in my junior clinics because the game is a popular sport for twelve-and-unders. "A golf drive is like a long kick, but a putt is more like a little pass to your teammate," I say. "Now imagine you are taking a penalty shot to win the game. You approach the ball from the side, and then you plant the front foot, swing the trailing right foot in an arc, and fire. You can't kick when your weight is on your back foot. In golf, you can't hit when your weight rests on your back foot either. In soccer, you must kick through the ball and finish with a nice follow-through. In golf, you must hit through the ball with a long follow-through."

Here are some parallels to golf from other sports and outdoor activities:

Frisbee Throwing

The motion of throwing a Frisbee is similar to the wind up of the golf swing. It's good practice for a right-handed person to throw the Frisbee with the left hand, since this is similar to what the left arm must do during a golf swing. (Lefties can use their right hands.)

Baseball

You would think that a baseball swing and a golf swing would have many similarities, but there are important differences. The bat is already back in baseball, while a golf swing starts with taking the club back and then swinging through. The batter must react to the pitcher's delivery; the golfer can hit anytime he wants. The grips are fundamentally different also: in baseball the bat is held in the palms of the hands, and in golf the grip is held in the fingers.

Despite the differences, however, the follow-through is very important in both golf and baseball. A "checked swing" won't get the ball out of the infield, and a checked swing in golf won't push the ball fifty yards down the fairway.

Hockey

Fortunately, golfers don't bodycheck others as they work their way down the fairway, but hockey is played with different sticks just as golf is played with different clubs. A goalie wields a stick with a big head and a big handle to deflect shots, and the goalie stick is designed for short pushes—not slap shots. The hockey slap spot is certainly similar to its golfing cousin—the big drive—as both are circular swings meant to crush the puck or ball.

Skiing

When you start skiing, ski instructors help first-time beginners make a wedge with their skis so they can brake on the snow. A *wedge,* get it? Seriously, have you ever noticed that kids have no fear on the slopes? They aren't afraid of falling or trying something new, and they trust their instructors.

In the same way, kids have no fear when they are one hundred yards out and have to hit over water to land on the green. They trust their swing to carry the ball there. If your kids are fearless on the course, know that that is entirely natural. Just let them go for it!

7

MRS. VANDERGOLF, I PRESUME

T he word *etiquette* may sound like a holdover from the Victorian Age, but this French word refers to codes governing correct behavior. You won't find any of the following forms of conduct written in the Rules of Golf, but they have been handed down from generation to generation, and every golfer *knows* them. Or at least they should. Abiding by golf etiquette won't improve a score, but it will make your children welcome on any golf course. That's a noble goal.

Golf etiquette begins on the practice tee and practice green. Neither area is a place for boorish behavior; loud talking disturbs other players trying to warm up or work the kinks out of their game. You don't have to be as quiet as a church mouse, but the practice tee should be treated with respect. On the practice green, use no more than three balls when putting. No running or boisterous outbursts, please.

On the first tee, decide who will hit first. If you are playing from the back tees while the kids are shooting from a forward set, then they must wait next to your tee box until you've hit. This reinforces a rule of etiquette: you should never stand in front of a player about to strike the ball. In addition, pull carts should be kept off tee boxes.

It's fine to talk and have fun as you play golf, but when a player is ready to hit, all chatter should cease. No one likes listening to another conversation while in the middle of the backswing. Players are encouraged to compliment each other's good shots, but thankfully, trash talking doesn't have a place in golf.

When your children tee off, remind them to watch where their ball lands. If your son notices that his ball bounced next to the tallest tree on the right side, he will have a much better chance of finding it. If he doesn't learn to follow the flight of the ball, his odds of locating a missing ball diminish.

Searching for lost balls—and there will be many over the course of a round—can be a frustrating experience. Your children should play with old balls, so when they knock them into the water or out of bounds, it's no big deal to leave them behind. What *is* a big deal is holding up the group playing behind you. They will become infuriated if they can't hit while you're using your ball retriever to lift Missy's ball from the bottom of the pond. Allow them to play through. If no one is playing behind you, however, you can take your time searching for Missy's errant shot.

The point you want to get across to your children is that golfers play without delay and play to a certain tempo, and that tempo involves walking to your ball, taking a practice swing or two, and hitting it. The furthest player out always hits first, and everyone else should stand out of range. No one should move, talk, or stand behind another golfer when he is addressing the ball. If you're riding in a cart that has to stay on the cart path, have your children take two or three clubs with them as they walk out to the ball so they don't have to run back to the cart to find their club of choice.

Slow play is the bane of today's golf—kind of like a long, windy sermon. If you don't like waiting to hit before every shot, then think about the group behind you: Are they standing by their bags casually swinging a club back and forth while they wait for *your group* to hit away? Six-hour rounds will dampen anyone's interest, especially kids with short attention spans.

As you walk down the fairway, have your children spread out as they walk toward their ball. The furthest one from the hole hits first. If the kids are big enough to make divots, they should retrieve the swatch of grass and tamp it back into the divot, or they should fill the divot with a sand-and-seed mixture provided by the club. Picking up trash along the way teaches them also to care for the course and keep it beautiful.

As you approach the green (where another foursome is holing out), allow the kids to hit if they can't reach the green. This keeps play moving so you won't hold up the group behind you. When approaching the green, you should pull your hand-carts and leave them where you will be exiting the green toward the next hole. Don't expect your children to be anticipating where the next tee box is, however, so ask them to follow you to the right place. Another no-no is pulling your cart between the green and a sand bunker.

If they land in the bunker, have them take the rake with them into the bunker. That way, they can smooth the sand as they exit the bunker. If they are in a bunker or just off the green, they should take their clubs *and* putter with them so they don't have to make two trips to their bags.

In a Fashion

Golf etiquette actually begins *before* you arrive at the golf course, and that involves what you and your children wear when you play golf.

I would be the first to agree that golf "fashion" over the years has had its lighter moments. I wince when I see video clips from the late '60s and early '70s of players sporting bell-bottomed slacks imprinted with paisley patterns and trimmed with two-inch-wide white belts and buck-white shoes—and I was one of those players! Some of our pants looked like a wild brushfire, and the lime-green shirts . . .

We used to joke that the reason people play golf is so they can wear clothes that they would not be caught dead in otherwise. Thankfully, those days are past. Golfers today play in some sharp-looking duds—monogrammed polo shirts, khaki Dockers, and stylish golf shoes. That's why I urge you and your children to make a reasonable attempt to dress the part. If your son or daughter walks to the first tee in a T-shirt (except at the most humble municipal courses), you may find yourself slapping your Visa card on the pro shop counter and docking yourself $39.95 plus tax for a new shirt.

Even if a course allows T-shirts, I urge you to have your kids wear a collared shirt. It will help them *feel* like they are playing golf. So will wearing their ball caps forward. It's been joked that anyone who turns his cap around automatically lowers their IQ by fifty points—and it certainly doesn't lower a handicap—so ask them to point the bill forward. Also, ditch the baggy pants or shorts. "Sagging" on the golf course looks as out of place as Speedo swim trunks. The same goes for blue jeans.

If you are new to the game, dressing up might feel a little funny at the outset, but after a while, you and the kids will like looking sharp.

Once they are safely on the green, show them how to fix plug marks—yours and others that have been left behind. They might think it's cool to push the two-pronged ball-mark repair tool into the green and fix the plug mark.

You should also give your kids a ball marker so they can get used to marking their balls. Again, the furthest one out putts first, unless someone is just off the green; they are allowed to hit, even though they are closer, since they have the option of hitting with the flagstick in. Once everyone is on the "dance floor" or putting surface, have one of your children pull out the flagstick and place it gently on the green and away from the hole.

If your ball marker is on the line of another's putt, ask whether he wants your marker moved. If you hit a lag putt within a foot of the hole, ask the group if you can finish; otherwise, mark your ball. Teach your children to walk *around* the line of someone waiting to putt. It's considered rude to trample on someone's line.

Keep things moving on the green. Yes, you want your children to study the slope of the green and correctly judge the speed, but they don't have to hitch their pants and hold up their putters like a plumb line for two minutes either. Keep the pace up without rushing everyone.

Once the last person has holed out, let your youngster replace the flagstick, but show her how to put the stick straight in the hole. You don't want her to bend the grassy rim while she sticks in the flagstick.

If another group is waiting to hit or is walking up the fairway, don't stand on the green analyzing the hole or counting up the strokes. Instead, step off the green and walk your pull carts to the next tee box, where you can write down scores and discuss any postmortems.

Final Thought

I know I've written a lot of do's and don'ts in this chapter, so I'm not expecting you to teach all this etiquette the first time out. But I will say this: if etiquette is taught early, it will not have to be reinforced as often.

Good etiquette not only ensures a pleasant golfing experience for you and your children, but also for the foursome behind you. If your children are wreaking havoc on the course, having a course marshal interrupt your game or having the local golf pro intercept your group at the eighteenth hole can make for an unpleasant exchange. Spare yourself and your youngsters an embarrassing reprimand by course marshals or icy glares from club members by following these rules of behavior.

When you get right down to it, good etiquette is a distilled version of the Golden Rule: Do unto others as you would have them do unto you.

8

LOTS OF RULES, JUST RIGHT

Is it just me, or have you noticed how many major corporations have commissioned advertising campaigns trumpeting the breaking of rules? Burger King told us, "Sometimes, you gotta break the rules," while Outback Steakhouse ("No rules. Just right."), Neiman Marcus ("No rules here"), Don Q rum ("Break all the rules"), and even an NFL video game ("No refs, no rules, no mercy") expound the antisocial theme that rules are a drag on life.

These ad slogans cause me to grind my teeth because I have a different worldview—one based on God's standards that contribute to social good and community order. For instance, God reserves sexual activity for a man and woman married to each other. God didn't do this because he doesn't want single persons to have any fun, but because he knows that sex within the bonds of marriage often produces offspring—little golfers—who need to be cared for, loved, and nurtured. It stands to reason that couples who've made the commitment to marry each other also have a strong commitment to raise their children in the context of a loving family.

What does this have to do with golf? A lot. Teaching your children the rules of golf—at the appropriate age and skill level—will teach them respect for the game *and* for other rules and boundaries they will encounter later in life, including, I dare say, the boundary line against premarital sexual activity.

Having said that, what would be the best way for your children to learn the rules of golf? Pick the right answer:

1. By signing them up for a two-day "Rules of the Game" course given twice a year by the local U.S. Golf Association chapter.
2. Through trial and error. Isn't that how you learned?
3. By handing them an official USGA Rules booklet and saying, "Here, read this. I'll quiz you in a week."
4. Rules? Who needs rules?
5. By teaching them the rules as situations present themselves on the golf course.

The correct answer, of course, is number 5, although a delicate balance must be offered here. Kids resent when we slip into our "lecture voice" and begin pounding rule after rule into their brains. You know, the kind of voice that sounds like a sermon is coming.

Rule teaching has to appear as natural as commenting about the weather or about the chances of the Chicago Cubs winning a National League pennant. Before

---

When Do You Start Playing by the Rules?

I love this question because when the kids are just starting to play, you *can't* play by all the rules. For instance, I think it's better for very young players to start from the 150-yard or 200-yard markers, tee up the ball for each shot, and disregard the score. Mulligans, or taking shots over, can be granted liberally.

You will have to make the decision how to teach and enforce the rules, based upon the child's skill level and desire to play the game. If Carissa and Toby are just starting out, and it's a coin toss whether they can put a clubface on the ball, I'm going to be doing everything I can to make golf the greatest experience since the Ringling Brothers and Barnum & Bailey Circus last came into town. If that means it's Mulligan City out there, then so be it.

On the other hand, I'm a great believer in the sanctity of golf and its rich history as a self-managed game that adheres to a strict code of rules and ethics. If your children become serious about the game (want to keep score, play in a junior tournament, etc.), the time has come to play by the rules.

As painful as this adjustment can be, they will be better off in the long run playing under the pressure of knowing that every shot counts. No mulligans, no second chances. Sooner rather than later, they need to understand that once the swing is made, they must live with the result—good, bad, or ugly.

you can teach your children about rules, however, you must know what you're talking about.

Golf has thirty-four main rules and a bushel of appendixes that cover everything from double hits to jackrabbits running off with your ball. While I can't expect you to memorize all the rules, having a cursory knowledge will help you play the game as it should be played and increase your enjoyment. Knowing the rules might even *save* you strokes.

Consider what happened to Arnold Palmer at the 1958 Masters. Arnie was making one of his patented final round charges, and "Arnie's Army" of fans were cheering him on. As he entered Augusta National's "Amen Corner" on the back nine, Arnie held a slim, one-stroke lead on the field.

On the par-3 twelfth hole, Palmer's tee shot failed to make the green. The ball landed in muddy grass and sunk halfway into the ground. A rules official dispatched to the scene ruled that Arnie had to play the nearly buried ball as it lay, but Arnie argued that the players had been told they could lift and drop their ball without penalty due to heavy rains the previous evening. The players were not allowed a free drop, however, if their balls landed in a sand trap, water hazard, or putting green.

Since his ball was in the grass just off the green, Arnie pleaded that he was entitled to pick up the ball, clean it, and take a free drop, but the rules official was adamant: play it where it lies. Arnie obeyed, and all he could do with his wedge was advance the ball eighteen inches. Then he chipped onto the green and took his two putts for a double-bogey 5.

Then Arnie had a great idea. Because he was *sure* he was right, he returned to the spot where his tee shot had become embedded in the soft mud, dropped a provisional ball over his shoulder, and replayed the hole. This time he got up and down, chipping close to the hole and knocking in a clutch one-putt for a par-3.

Several holes later, Arnie was vindicated when tournament officials ruled that he was right. The Rules of Golf entitled Arnie to play a provisional ball and get a ruling from the rules director later on. When he received the good news, Arnie penciled in a 3 for number 12, which gave him a clubhouse lead on the field. Ten contenders took shots at his 284 total score, but they all fell short. Since Arnie had saved himself two precious shots on number 12, he captured the 1958 Masters by a single stroke!

The Rules

Although it's doubtful you'll run into a situation like Arnold Palmer did at Augusta, it's not enough to say, "We're still playing winter rules, so I get a free drop" during a Memorial Day weekend golf outing with your kids. Although I can't cover every rule in this book, let me highlight some important ones by using a question-and-answer format.

Q: Why does golf have so many rules?

Uncle Wally: The quick answer is that many situations come up where you need a rule book to help you figure out what to do next. Listen, rules aren't written to hassle you but to help you make the right (and fair) ruling. Rules help you play the game in a fun way and provide structure and order. As I illustrated with Arnold Palmer's story, if you know the rules, you can use them to *help* you. A few years ago, Tiger Woods was playing a desert course at the Phoenix Open when he hit an errant tee shot behind a wheelbarrow-sized sandstone boulder. Because the rock was a "loose impediment" (according to the rule book), he could have it moved. The rock was too big for him and his caddie to move, so he employed some bystanders to push the boulder out of his way. Clever thinking, Tiger!

Another rule states that you must play the ball where it lies, but let's say that you hit an errant ball into the woods. You find your Titleist ball behind a tree or a bush. This is not the time to kick the ball into a clearing when no one is looking; you must take your medicine and either accept a one-stroke penalty for having an unplayable lie in a hazard, or you have to play it where you found it.

Honesty is a great value to have in your bag. The trouble for most folks, as author F. M. Hubbard once said, is that "honesty pays, but it doesn't seem to pay enough to suit some people." I've learned the lesson that honesty is a virtue worth paying for, even if it costs you a few strokes or a friendly competition. What's more, it's biblical. "Dishonest scales are detestable to the LORD, but an accurate weight

---

The Tough Lessons of Life

Golf teaches lessons not taught anywhere else, and they can be painful. One of my most difficult times with Scott was the time he was playing an important high school match for Orangewood Christian School. I was following Scott one afternoon when he sliced a drive way off to the left. The ball wasn't out of bounds, but it was in the bottom of a dry riverbed, or what is known in the rules books as a hazard.

Scott took his 5-iron and walked into the hazard, surveyed his options, then lined up to hit. I noticed he grounded his club behind the ball, just as everyone grounds a club in the fairway before striking the ball. What Scott didn't know was that playing the ball in the hazard was just like playing the ball from a sand bunker—you can't ground the club before making the swing.

When Scott finished his round, I asked him what he marked down for that hole.

"I had a four, Dad. Saved par."

"No, you had a five."

"A five?"

"Yes, a five. You have to count a stroke when you ground a club in the hazard."

All the color drained from Scott's face when he realized what he had done. But it got worse. Adding a stroke to his scorecard resulted in his team losing the match instead of tying. At first, Scott was really mad at me. I suppose I would have been, too, had I been a teenager. But after a few days, he saw the wisdom of what I had done and came around to my point of view.

I can tell you one thing: Scott never grounded his club in a hazard again.

---

is His delight," says Proverbs 11:1 (HCSB), which in golf terms could be rewritten to say, "The Lord abhors dishonest scorecards, but accurate ones are his delight."

Q: What's the most important rule to know?

Uncle Wally: It is most important to know when you're inbounds and when you are out of bounds. Most holes are lined with stakes, and those boundaries mean different things based upon the color of the stakes.

- *White stakes* mean the ball is out of bounds (OB). If you hit from the tee and sail the ball OB, you lose a stroke and the distance you hit. In other words, hit another ball from the tee, and the next ball you hit will be your third shot. (Bummer!) The same goes for a shot from the fairway. Hit OB, and you're penalized a stroke and distance.

- *Yellow stakes* define a water hazard. The options you have are
  1. play the ball where it lies. Always be careful in any hazard, whether it is a sand trap or water hazard, to not touch the water or the ground or sand within the hazard. If you do, it is a one-stroke penalty.
  2. replay the shot from its original place, adding one penalty stroke.
  3. keep the spot where the ball last crossed the hazard between you and the hole, then you may go back as far as you like and drop, adding a one-stroke penalty to your score.
- *Red stakes* define a lateral water hazard. You may select any one of the three water hazard options or choose two more options. These are
  1. drop a ball within two club lengths from the point where the ball crossed the hazard line but not nearer the hole, adding one stroke to your score.
  2. go to a point on the other side of the hazard the same distance from the hole and drop a ball within two club lengths, adding one stroke to your score.

Q: Jason, my teenager, can hit the ball hard, but he can be wild. Last week he airmailed the ball onto the wrong green. We didn't know what to do, but I figured the golf course didn't want him taking a divot on a fragile green, so I told him to move the ball. Was I right?

Uncle Wally: As long as he placed the ball to the nearest edge no closer to the hole, you did the right thing.

Q: How many clubs can I carry?

Uncle Wally: Fourteen, so leave that 4-wood, 7-wood, 1-iron, and A-wedge at home. Kids ten and under don't need that many clubs, and they shouldn't get used to carrying many clubs onto the course. Another thing: if you intentionally break a club during play, you can't replace it.

Q: Can I hit a moving ball?

Uncle Wally: No, you must wait until the ball comes to a halt—even if you're in a trap and flub a sand shot. Wait until the ball stops rolling. That rule also applies on putts.

Q: I recently hit my ball into a creek with one inch of standing water. Is it always an automatic one-stroke penalty for hitting into the water?

Uncle Wally: No. You can play where it lies; if you think you can get the ball onto dry land, take a whack at it. For that matter you can hit a ball lying in six inches of water if you want, although 99.99 percent of the time you won't get the ball out of the hazard. You're usually better off taking a one-stroke penalty.

Q: How do I drop a ball?

Uncle Wally: Do so very carefully because you want your ball to "sit up" as much as possible. You should mark where your ball entered the hazard with a tee, measure two club lengths back, stand over the area, and drop the ball from shoulder height at arm's length.

Q: What if my dropped ball rolls back into the water? Tough luck?

Uncle Wally: Don't be ridiculous. The rules stipulate you can redrop without penalty. If the ball comes to rest more than two club lengths from where you entered the hazard, however, then you are entitled to a redrop.

Q: What if I redrop and the ball keeps rolling more than two club lengths?

Uncle Wally: Then you get to place the ball nicely and gently on the hilly terrain on the spot where it first struck the ground when you redropped.

Q: My son and I aren't that precise with our preshot routine and "waggles." Sometimes I lightly tap the ball when it is on the tee, knocking it off the tee a couple of inches. I didn't mean to hit it. Does it still count as a stroke?

Uncle Wally: That's a freebie. You can put the ball back on the tee without penalty. Even if you start a real swing but abort at the last second—knocking the ball off the tee—you can replace your ball.

Q: My shots always head for the cart paths. What kind of relief do I get?

Uncle Wally: A lot. If the ball is lying on a paved cart path, you can drop it to the nearest point on the grass as long as you are no closer to the hole. You have to be within one club length, however. If the ball is on the grass but your stance has you standing on the paved cart path, you get relief. You also get a free drop when your ball lands next to electrical boxes, sprinkler control boxes, sprinkler heads, and "permanent" on-course structures such as wells and rest rooms.

Q: I hear all these weird rules about "burrowing animals" and how you can get free relief. What's the rule?

Uncle Wally: If your ball rolls down a rabbit hole, you're in luck: no penalty. If a rabbit—or the neighborhood dog—takes off with your ball you can also play a

---

A Teutonic Terror

This is one of my favorite stories about honesty on the golf course. It seems that a foursome was looping a wonderful course just outside Stuttgart, Germany. They came upon one of the course's toughest holes—an 185-yard par-3 with an elevated green.

Hans had honors with this foursome. He stepped up to the tee, took out a 5-wood, and munched a drive toward the elevated green. The ball sailed beyond the green and into the forest. The rest of the group punched their woods onto the green's apron.

When the foursome arrived at the green, they began looking for Hans's ball.

They searched the bunkers and rough. Nothing. They used their wedges to push back the shrubs ringing the green, but again his ball couldn't be found. As his three playing partners were poking around, Hans nonchalantly took a ball out of his pocket and dropped it five yards off the green.

"*Ja, Ich habe den Ball gefunden,*" Hans yelled out, happy that he wasn't OB. He chipped on to the green, as did his friends.

But something interesting happened when one of his friends pulled the pin. There was a ball already in the cup. Hans had holed his tee shot!

That was the last day Hans was president of the Stuttgart Golf Club.

---

substitute ball without penalty. But don't expect to get away with ruling an ant as a "burrowing animal" and getting relief from a tiny ant hole, unless they are fire ants, located in the southeastern United States.

Q: I've noticed that once the pros reach the green, they hand the ball to their caddies for them to clean. Can I clean the ball when it gets dirty on the fairway?

Uncle Wally: No, unless you are playing "lift, clean, and place" rules, which happens after a heavy rainfall and the course is flooded. Under normal conditions, you have to play a dirty ball until you reach the green, where you can clean it before putting.

Q: My son and I always forget which ball we're playing with, and it doesn't help matters when he pulls another Titleist from a sleeve of balls in my bag. Does it really matter if he hits my ball once in a while?

Uncle Wally: Hitting the wrong ball is a two-shot penalty, and one that can be easily avoided. Keep an indelible Marks-a-Lot in your bag and have each of you put an identification mark on your balls. Let your kids get real creative with their own ID marks.

Q: What's the silliest rule?

Uncle Wally: The silliest rule is that you can't tell others what club you hit. That's considered "giving advice," which is disallowed according to the rules of golf.

This brings us to an interesting point about all these rules. According to the rule book, helping your daughter decide between an 8-iron and a 9-iron is against the rules, but that defeats the purpose of playing together. Yes, rules are very important. They are the bedrock of the game, and few PGA pros knew the rules better than I did when I played on the tour.

My point is this: enforcing every rule in the book while your children are just starting to play is counterproductive. Until your child is ready to play tournament golf or is entering the maturing teen years, emphasize the fun of golf more than the rules. When he or she becomes competitive, then you and the kids should take the weekend rules course from the USGA.

THE FIRST TEE SHOT

Still, no matter how well you know the rules, something goofy will happen. One time, I was playing the San Diego tour stop at Torrey Pines, a wonderful seaside course in La Jolla, California. I was finishing on the North course, a long par-5. I snaphooked my second shot past some trees and into a chain-link fence where a parking lot was located.

I found my ball lodged between the bottom of the fence and some porous blacktop. Since the fence was a permanent structure, I sought relief. To be sure, I called for a tournament official.

Meanwhile, my playing partners were anxious to finish and get to the clubhouse, so they played on. I watched several threesomes pass while I waited for an official. I remember Jack Nicklaus waving and laughing at my predicament.

When an official finally arrived on the scene, he ruled that I could *not* have relief from the fence, which frosted me. I picked up a club and walked over to the fence, wondering if I could somehow get a club on the ball.

While lost in my thoughts, I heard a voice say, "Why don't you come over here and hit the ball?"

Who said that?

I looked up and saw a bearded, hippielike character dressed in a dirty blue T-shirt and beige shorts on the other side of the fence, leaning against one of the cars in the parking lot. This fellow was saving a buck by watching the tournament from beyond the fence.

"If you came over here, you could pop that ball, no problem," the hippie said.

"You know, you just may be right."

A crowd had gathered around me, including a photographer from the *San Diego Union* newspaper, and they cheered me on as I climbed the chain-link fence, cleats and all. My caddie handed me my pitching wedge, and I inspected my lie.

I can get a club on this.

I tried taking a practice swing, but I couldn't draw the club halfway back before it hit the bumper of an old Pontiac.

"I can't put a full swing on it," I said to no one in particular.

"Wait a minute," said the hippie. "I think I can help you."

78

He walked over to the offending car, jimmied the front door, busted it open, and put it in neutral. Then he rolled the Pontiac back several feet so I could take a full swing.

This created an even bigger hubbub, and I knew I had to get out of there. I stepped up to the ball, waggled twice, and slammed the club into the bottom of the fence. The ball punched out in the direction of the green, and I settled for a bogey six. I like to tell people that I topped Tiger by moving a Pontiac instead of a boulder.

Q: What do you think about gambling on the course?
Uncle Wally: Some say that betting and golf go together like chocolate sauce and vanilla ice cream, and there's no doubt that golfers have been making friendly wagers since the days of the gutta-percha balls back in the nineteenth century.

I can't think of too many golfers—even my Christian buddies—who haven't played at one time or another for something more than pride. Sometimes a small wager works as an incentive to play well. Lee Trevino, a Hispanic who grew up in a cold-water shack and taught himself the game as an eight-year-old caddy, said you don't know what pressure is until you're playing for five bucks with only two in your pocket.

Having said that, there's a world of difference between playing for who buys Cokes in the clubhouse versus high-stakes gambling with hundreds, if not thousands, of dollars riding on each hole. Basketball star and golf nut Michael Jordan, according to numerous sources, has won and lost hundreds of thousands of dollars on a single round of golf.

Gambling must be approached very carefully because it is addictive and progressive. If you *must* have something riding on every round—even if it's just a few bucks—then I would say that you have a problem. If you occasionally have to pay for your Saturday morning foursome's refreshments after the game, then it's no big deal.

Although you won't find any "thou shalt nots" in the Bible regarding "skins" or "wolf" games, Scripture isn't silent on the topic. The Bible says:
- Gambling encourages greed (Luke 12:15; Heb. 13:5; 1 Tim. 6:10).
- Gambling encourages materialism and discontent (1 Tim. 6:9; Ps. 62:10).

- Gambling discourages honest labor (Prov. 28:19; 13:11).
- Gambling encourages get-rich-quick thinking (Prov. 28:20).

As for me, I wouldn't gamble if I was playing in a friendly father-son foursome. It can bring a lot of unnecessary pressure and frayed tempers.

I never bet with my sons, but I sure gave them a lot of "incentives" to beat me. Scott, who loved the pressure of having to perform, won more banana splits from me than I care to remember.

The Worst-Case Scenario

After weeks of buildup, your eight-year-old son, Tommy, joins you for his first eighteen-hole excursion. You're walking the course. Two and a half hours into the round at number 12, he repeats the following statement for the fifth time in the last five minutes: "I'm tired, Dad. Can we go in?"

Go in? I paid ninety dollars for us to play today. Whaddya mean you want to go in?

That's what you're thinking. You're also wondering what your wife would say if you attack him with your ball mark repair tool. Swallow your pride, Dad. Wave *adios* to the money and head in.

I'm not saying you should give in to the first whine. You know your child best, which means you should be able to distinguish between petulant behavior and a genuine desire to call it quits.

Resist the temptation to say, "Tommy, you can pull your cart while I finish the round." You may gain a short-term victory and keep playing golf, but you will lose the war about whether he will get turned on to golf.

If you're riding in a cart and just have a few holes to play, you can probably finish out. When Blake was just starting out, I always asked him to bring along a book, portable CD player, or GameBoy in case he wanted to quit. As long as he could do something in the cart, he didn't mind if I finished my round. However, I always said, "Blake, if you want to play a hole, then let me know." He was usually content to play his hand-held video games, eat his candy, or grab a Coke from the cooler, but sometimes he wanted to play another hole after taking a break. One thing I learned early on was that I could not *make* Blake play just because his older brother could never get enough of the sport.

I can tell you another thing to avoid at all costs: having your nonplaying son or daughter ride with you for all eighteen holes. Unless your child is at an age where he or she is enamored with a golf cart, this is something akin to Chinese water torture for fidgety kids. They will grow up *hating* golf. Take my word for it.

9

TEEING IT UP

W hat's par, Dad?"

"Same as the last hole, Scott. Par for you would be five."

With hands on his hips, Scott surveyed the hole as he prepared to hit his tee shot. We stood in the middle of the fairway at the 150-yard markers. Scott set down a tee and pulled his trusty 3-wood from his bag. I had already hit my drive from the blue tips on this dogleg 383-yard par-4 hole, and my ball was resting about 25 yards closer to the hole.

Scott was six years old, and he reveled in playing an eighteen-hole regulation course for the first time. I had debated whether to start him from the ladies tees or even the junior tees, but I judged those distances as too far for his skill level. On all the par-4 and par-5 holes, I played from the blues and then drove the cart to the 150-yard markers, where Scott teed off.

Why did we play this way? The distance was right for his age and ability. He always had a good lie off the fairway and an unfettered shot open to the green. He was not overmatched at 150 yards out.

"You still owe me an ice cream, Dad," Scott said.

"I know, I know," I replied, raising my hands. Scott had "birdied" the last hole—a "par-5"—with a one-hundred-yard tee shot, a chip onto the green, a well-struck lag putt, and a two-footer into the back of the cup. Scott liked shooting for pars and birdies, and that's what I tried to do—set realistic goals for them. I had stumbled upon a pleasurable way for Scott to play golf.

Will our approach work for your children? You are the best arbiter of that. Your options are many: the children can start from the 100-, 150-, or 200-yard markers, or they can play from the junior or ladies tees. The idea is have them start from where they have a legitimate chance of making a par or bogey.

What you don't want to do is *make* them play the blue tees with you. If you're a good player and your thirteen-year-old son is just starting to hit the ball with some consistency, don't force him back to the blue tips; you are putting him on a course that he doesn't have the game for. Let him start from a point on the course where he can play. (Note: you should only be playing the blue tees if you are a 10-handicap player or better.)

Besides, there is more than one way to start a hole. If your children are teenagers and you're a high handicapper, why not play from the red tees? You'll both have fun scoring better. If you're playing from the back tees and your son insists on playing with the "big boys," let him play with you as long as he understands that he can hit his second shot from where *your* ball lands. (Keep it on the fairway, Dad!)

If your daughter's tee box is behind a water hazard, let her tee off from the side of the pond. She could become seriously disinterested in golf if shot after shot gets wet.

One thing I would insist upon with beginners is allowing them to tee up the ball on every shot. Let them place the ball on the tee as you work your way down the fairway, including the traps! (The ball is much more strikable when placed on a tee.) If they happen to hit into a bunker, give them one chance to get out, and if they are unsuccessful, let them remove the ball from the trap and put it on the green. Who cares? Remember, the goal is to have fun.

For some testosterone-laden teenage boys, having fun means borrowing your Callaway Great Big Bertha II driver and swinging with all their might off an elevated tee box. Don't let them windmill those drivers until they can hit a 5-wood and then a 3-wood. The late, great teaching pro Harvey Penick said that 90 percent of players should leave their drivers in the closet, and that applies to thirteen-year-old boys as well.

Many golfing parents forget how long eighteen holes take to play. Trust me, you'll spend five or six hours completing a round with a beginning child, that is too long for any child to stick with a new sport. No, it's better to bite off less and play nine holes for the first few times—even throughout the first year. You can try eighteen holes, but if your kids get cranky during the middle of the back nine, they could lose interest or start acting up. If that happens, it's time to go in.

To Score or Not to Score

'Tis a great question, and one worth pondering as long as Hamlet contemplated that other orb. Some kids will want their score kept, including number of putts. Others couldn't care less. For at least the first few times around the course, I would stash the four-inch pencil in your equipment bag. When the kids are taking eight, ten, twelve whacks a hole, scoring doesn't serve much purpose. But I'm all for scoring if the kids want a measuring stick that records their improvement. Watching their nine-hole score drop from 75 to 69 to 62 should encourage them to play and practice even more.

With Scott, I didn't focus on what number he shot but how he played against "par." I believed an artificial par number was easier to handle than the "snowmans" and double-digit numbers he would have scribbled on his scorecard.

Learn How to Walk

Unless you belong to a club where carts are mandatory, you should always walk the course with your children. Don't ask me why, but walking will teach your youngsters to appreciate the game more. Patience is a difficult concept to convey in this pop-it-in-a-microwave, order-at-the-drive-thru world, but your children will gain a measure of poise and equanimity from the few extra minutes it takes to walk to the next shot.

Walking teaches other things, as well. If your child is hitting to the left side of the fairway and then to right, she'll pick up on that. Finally, walking gives players more time to calm their nerves between shots. It's easier to deal with a duck hook into the trees after a five-minute walk than after a speedy ride to the scene of the crime.

Want more virtues? Walking is great exercise, allows for more conversation, and generally makes any parent-child round worth remembering.

When you do start keeping score, be prepared for some inventive counting.

Dad: "What did you have on the last hole, Matt?"

Eight-year-old Matt: "Uh, let's see. I know. It was a six."

"Six? Did you count all the times you hit the ball?"

"Yes, I did. It was a six, wasn't it?"

"Well, it took you three shots just to get out of that sand trap. Didn't you hit the ball three times before getting into the trap?"

"There was my drive, and then I hit it in the rough. Then . . . you're right, Dad."

"So you were in the sand with three shots, and it took you three to get out. How many shots do you now have?"

"Six."

"And then you putted how many times?"

"Three."

"No, it was four. I'm afraid you missed that tiny putt at the end."

"Oh, yeah."

"I'm afraid I have you with a ten."

Such conversations can be painful, but if you refrain from making a big deal out of it, you'll both shrug it off. You'll find that kids are eternal optimists when they add up their score for the hole. But there will come a time when your son or daughter will have to properly count strokes as part of their maturation. Without learning respect for what they shoot, they will not successfully enjoy the game as it was meant to be played. Keeping score means learning to squarely face the results of each swing.

Hail to the Thief

Former president Bill Clinton, who's so crazy about golf that he said his game actually improved while he was in office (now there's a scary thought), has become so famous for taking mulligans that they are called "billigans."

I've read numerous magazine articles about Clinton's penchant for "reloading" after hitting a shot that (a) went out of bounds, (b) was topped and didn't reach the women's tee, or (c) simply didn't go where he wanted. Remember, I don't have a problem with players taking mulligans if they're not keeping score, especially if they're not breaking 100. But if you *are* keeping score, then you have to accept the results of your shot. That's what golf is all about. Maybe Clinton felt a presidential prerogative to take reshots, but he shouldn't have announced to the White House press corps that he broke 80 for the first time when an actual count would have yielded a score closer to triple digits. Nor should he have bragged that he "plays to a 12 handicap," as he told one interviewer. *Yeah, and I can fly Air Force One.*

Don Van Natta Jr., in researching a book called *First Off the Tee: Presidential Hackers, Duffers, and Cheaters from Taft to Bush,* called President Clinton and asked whether he could play a round with him. Surely, Clinton understood why Van Natta asked to play eighteen holes with him—it would be a chapter in Van Natta's book. The former president agreed to meet the writer, a *New York Times* reporter with a 28-handicap, at a private club near his home in Chappaqua, New York.

What happened over their eighteen holes was a slew of "practice shots," retees, and gimme putts that were, let's say, well beyond twenty inches. A typical hole that Van Natta recounted was the par-4 fifth hole, where Clinton duck-hooked his drive into the trees. His second tee shot didn't go very far, so he reloaded a third time,

---

Some Golf Lingo You'll Probably Hear

If you're new to golf and turn on a golf broadcast, it can sound like you're eavesdropping on a game played on another planet. Sound bites like the following seem nearly indecipherable:

- "I'm surprised Tiger went with a five from the second-cut rough, but he wanted to reach this par-5 in two to have a chance at eagle."
- "Tap-in for par, but that really has to feel like a bogey to Sergio since he birdied this short dogleg par-4 in yesterday's round."
- "After his pin-high approach, Vijay is staring at a tricky, double-break putt. The stimpmeter on this green is 14 today, Jim. No one has read the speed or distance on this putt all afternoon."

Don't let the lingo throw you off. If you and your kids hang around golf long enough, you will pick up this stuff. You'll be talking about "chili dips" and "canaries" in no time.

hitting it long and far into the trees. Clinton drove toward ball 3 in his cart, where he found it and took a drop. That shot landed short of the green. From the fringe, Clinton took three more practice shots before playing the second one, which stayed on the green. Clinton then picked up without putting, and on his scorecard he wrote the number "4" for his score.

According to the card, President Clinton shot an 82 that day, but he was only fooling himself. Van Natta said the presidential duffer probably took two hundred swings that afternoon.

When to Hold 'Em, When to Fold 'Em

Let me assure you that I was never a spoilsport with my kids. When the wheels fell off for Blake—and I could see discouragement written all over his face—I got him a treat at the snack bar when we made the turn. Then on the number 10 tee, I said, "You know what, Blake? Let's play a two-man scramble on the back nine. Whichever one of us hits the better shot, we'll play from that one."

Blake loved that because if he was hitting from the 150-yard markers, he usually "outdrove" me since I had started back at the blues. That meant we played our second shot from his ball, which translated into lots of birdies on the scorecard. Blake enjoyed telling his friends that we went "really low."

It is important to keep in mind *when* you play golf with your children. Saturday morning at 9:00 A.M. in midsummer might not be the best time to have Michael and Mindy playing their first nine holes. You'll have fire-snorting foursomes breathing down your necks, and you'll feel the heat to keep everyone moving. You don't want impatient foursomes playing up your backs.

Instead, start in the late afternoon, when many courses are deserted. In the summertime, take advantage of the long days with a 6:00 P.M. tee time. That's plenty of time for nine holes.

Hey, Mr. Coach

Younger children need instruction and reminders and guidelines and hints. For instance, let's say your son hits into the woods and finds his ball. He could hit for a five-foot gap between two trees and try to reach the green, but he would have to thread a needle. Or, you could point out that if he pitches sideward back into the fairway, he is playing high percentage golf and can still get up and down if he hits a good approach shot.

Depending on the outcome, you'll probably have something to discuss. He may choose to play through the trees; if so, let him try because he has to learn a lesson. If he ricochets his shot through the woods like a steel ball in a pinball machine, don't talk to him about hitting dangerous shots until after the game. When the topic does come up, this could also give you an opening to make a spiritual point—that God wants us to look for the safest way to go through life, which is why he gave us his commands in the Bible. God's rules keep us safe.

> ### Starting Out Checklist
> Once your children have a good swing and can hit the ball competently, they are ready to play *real* golf.
> - Start with a par-3 course, preferably in the afternoon when play is less crowded.
> - Play nine holes, if possible.
> - Let the kids start at the 200-, 150-, or 100-yard markers, depending on their age and skill.
> - Don't bother keeping score the first couple of times out, but after that, give them a "par" to shoot for.
> - Realize that you will not be able to work on your own golf game. Just make sure they have fun.

Nonetheless, you must make the point that every round is comprised of good shots and bad shots, good breaks and horrible breaks. That's golf, which means we need to place our trust in God, who can be depended upon to be a steady influence in our lives.

The thing *not* to do is to go into teaching guru David Leadbetter mode, critiquing every twitch and waggle.

"I see parents all over their kids, telling them they moved their heads, swung too fast, didn't grip the club right, stuff like that," says golf pro Bobby McIver. "Those overenthusiastic parents are frustrating their kids by overcoaching on the course. Your good intentions are working against them. Kids learn by mistakes—and parents learn that way too. It's OK if a kid misses a golf shot. It's just a golf shot."

10

THE LONG AND SHORT OF IT

Golf is really a game within a game, and what I'm referring to is the long game versus the short game. Let me illustrate this concept. Everyone's heard the old adage, "You drive for show and putt for dough," but there's a lot that happens in between because very few players—even the par-busting pros—are skilled enough to regularly hit the ball on the green in regulation.

"In regulation" means knocking the ball on the putting surface in one shot on a par-3, two shots on a par-4, and three shots on a par-5. When balls land just off the green, the challenge is to "turn three shots into two," as golfing great Bobby Jones once said. Developing a good short game that gobbles up extra strokes in a hurry does this.

Many parents make the mistake of trying to teach their kids the long game first. They walk out to the driving range and hand their kids an old driver and watch them flail away with the most frustrating club in the bag. Actually, it's far better to start kids by letting them putt near the hole and then work up to chip shots from the fringe just off the green.

Earl Woods, Tiger's father, said in his book *Training a Tiger,* "I firmly believe that in order to teach the full golf swing, you must start with the simplest golf swing—the putt—and then move on to chipping and pitching. Golf should be taught from the green back to the tee."

I can add my amen to that, and here's another reason why I feel so strongly about it: a bad player with a good short game is always going to beat a good player with a poor short game. Finesse around the greens and a solid putting stroke are the calling cards of low-handicap players. The booming drive can always come later. Besides, the short game is where your smaller youngsters can shine because size and age are mitigated. The short game is where Davids reign and Goliaths fall.

The next time you take your kids out to the chipping green, drop a few balls about twenty to forty yards from the green and then take one in your hand. "Jennifer, see this ball? I'm going to throw this ball on the green."

Then take your arm back and throw the ball on the green. Have your children do the same.

"Kids, here's one thing you should know. Nearly two-thirds of all golf shots are within a toss to the hole. Only one-third of golf is getting the ball to this point. That's how important the short game is in golf."

I'll give you another reason why the short game is so important. When Tiger Woods burst into America's living rooms, what was he known for? Answer: his booming drives and out-of-this world length that reduced 550-yard par-5s to toothless holes that could be easily reached in two shots. When Tiger's game faltered a few years ago, golf pundits whispered that Tiger's short game was betraying him time and time again. They were right, and Tiger knew it. What impresses me about this story is that Tiger did something about it.

Tiger enlisted swing coach Butch Harmon, a former tour player, to retool his short game. For months, either at Harmon's golf academy or at tournaments, the pair spent hours on the practice tee laboriously hitting balls and analyzing Tiger's swing on tapes and a computer.

Butch worked on Tiger getting the clubface slightly less closed on the top of the backswing, which allowed Tiger to "hold on" a bit longer at contact. I know we are getting very technical here, but this fundamental change in Tiger's swing allowed him better control over his trajectory and gave him laserlike accuracy on shots to the green.

"It's a lot of hitting balls to the point where your hands are so sore that you don't want to do anything the next day," Tiger told an interviewer with *Golf Digest* magazine. I'm willing to bet that Tiger thinks all the hard work was worth it; he captured the "Tiger Slam" by holding all four majors titles at one time—the Masters, the U.S. Open, the British Open, and the PGA.

But here's a quote that should inspire us all. Butch Harmon said, "Tiger practices three times as much on his short game as his long game."

Did you catch that? Tiger devotes three hours to pitches, chips, and sand shots for every hour he launches moon shots from the practice tee. If Tiger can do that, so can we.

The first thing we need to do is change our mind-set. Think of the short game as hitting the ball one inch to twelve thousand inches (or one inch to one hundred yards). Ready to get started? Let's start with putting.

Putting

Anyone, and I mean anyone, can bump the ball with a putter—and it's fun. That's why "putt-putt" or miniature golf courses are filled with tottering grandparents and rambunctious grandkids trying to putt the ball past the twirling windmill.

The putting stroke is a simple back-and-forth pendulum motion that feels like a miniswing. One way to understand this short stroke is to employ two training aids: a thin book and a plastic clothes hanger.

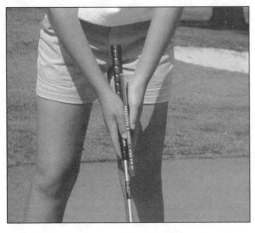

The book helps youngsters realize that the hands work in concert while the wrists stay firm. The biggest mistake I see with young putters is their propensity to "break" their wrists as they strike the ball, which lessens their ability to control the speed of the putt. Place a thin book between their hands, and then have them make a puttinglike swing while keeping the book firmly between their hands. This shows them that the wrists do not break.

I also like using a plastic clothes hanger because it helps them keep the putter-face square to the target. Have your children place their arms inside a plastic hanger and then putt. This will show them how the arms stay together in a pendulum. This

feeling is worth a million dollars. From there, putting is all about dealing with two variables—line and distance. If they hit the ball on their line and have the right speed, they will make the putt.

Good putting starts with the proper grip. I teach the traditional grip, which is the dominant hand underneath (right hand for right-handed players). You need a good feel when you grip the club, and if a baseball grip does that for you, then go for it. The grip should be no firmer than holding a pencil or taking the club out of your bag.

If you are a cross-handed putter and want your kids to learn that putting style, I have no problem with that. Do whatever works, and apparently cross-handed works on the PGA Tour, where Jim Furyk and Fred Couples are the most noted practitioners.

Nevertheless, putting has rituals that kids should learn before they draw the blade back:

1. Have your children stand with their eyes over the ball with putters that are not too short or too long. A club pro can help you make the proper judgment.
2. Evenly distribute their weight between their feet. Their stance should be comfortable and natural, with knees slightly bent. Have them make one practice stroke from behind the ball.
3. Have your children set the clubface square to the target and ask them to decide on the line and speed of the putt. Then step behind your youngster and check to see how the putter is lined up. The ball should be positioned in the center of the putter.
4. The putting stroke is like a pendulum: just a little back, but the follow-through is free. Have the children imagine that the bottom of the putter is a brush and direct them to brush the grass back and forth, as if they are painting a line on the green. With the pendulum, they should imagine that their hands and the club are the hands of a clock. Have them say "Tick" on the back swing and "Tock" on the forward. This will give them a nice rhythm when they putt.
5. Have your child hit the center of the ball—not the top or the bottom—in one consistent stroke. The putt is a delicate shot.
6. A good image for kids to have is that of an elephant swinging its trunk back and forth. They should keep this picture in their minds when they are making their strokes back and forth. Have them pretend that they are an elephant swinging their trunk as they putt.

Fun Drills

The following are some of the most creative drills that I have used in my teaching, and you can do these with your kids. Purchase some of the training tools at your local hardware store or toy store, and then have some fun with the kids. You can do the drills right along with your kids. They will really like that. It may even sharpen up your own game.

Path—String Carpet

Having a good image in putting is so critical. Putting down a line is limited, but when you set up this drill, you will help the kids to imagine a four-inch-wide carpet or bowling alley. You will be surprised how many putts they can make in a row when they are not trying to putt down a line.

Use two strings to make a "bowling alley" to the hole. Place two tees just behind the cup's edge, then stretch the string around the hole forming a carpet to roll the ball down to the hole. You may wish to tighten the carpet to two inches wide for a real challenge. This drill will help you swing the putterface straight back and straight through.

Direction—Striped Ball Drill

Draw lines or stripes with a magic marker on some practice balls. Then line them up in the direction that you want the ball to roll. If your putter has a line on the top edge, you may wish to

line this up with the stripe on the ball. Then roll the ball end over end like rolling a tire down the street. Many of the pros put lines on their balls when they play or they line up the name brand in the direction that they wish the ball to roll. This is one concept that you can take from the practice green on to the course.

Distance Control and Touch— Wire Wickets

Take pipe cleaners or wire and build little wickets on the green. You may wish to place them in a straight line and space them as it is shown in the picture. Have the child stroke down the tunnel into the cup. Make the row as long or as short as you want. As they putt down their little tunnels, they will hopefully be able to carry this image on to the golf course.

You may even wish to have a competitive game and set up your pipe cleaner wickets as a small croquet course. Putt through the first wicket, then go for the second. Just like in croquet, if you miss a wicket you have to come back around and through. The final wicket is next to the cup. Instead of hitting the croquet post to finish out, you putt into the cup.

Distance Awareness—Stairs with Clubs

To learn how to putt for distance, stagger several golf clubs on the green. Get a feeling for distance by putting one ball between the first and second club, second and third club, and so on. This is like putting up "stairs."

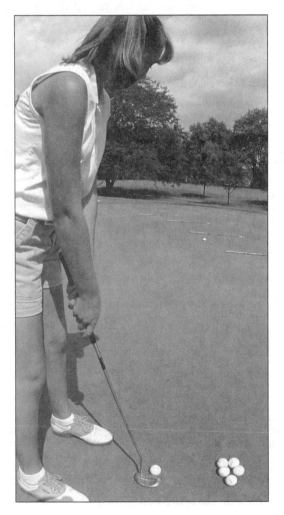

Pendulum Feeling—Yardstick

Mark a yardstick in different increments as shown in the pictures on the next page. Then set up your yardstick, aiming just to the left of the hole parallel to your target line so that the putter blade can swing right alongside the yardstick. Then have your child practice pendulum stroking, always taking the

blade back to a certain point and forward the same distance from the center point. As she begins to putt this way, she will feel how much arm swing is required to roll the ball certain distances. She will also develop a consistent pendulum motion, which is so needed for good putting.

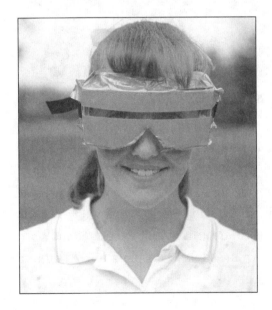

Eye Alignment—Goggles

For this drill all you need is a pair of safety goggles or old ski goggles and duct tape or masking tape. Put the tape on the safety goggles so that your eyes are in line with the target line, and you line up your putt.

If your eyes are aimed out to the right, your arms will have a tendency to swing out in that direction. As you can see from the picture on the next page, I am aiming a flagstick straight to the hole. When my student looks down, she will see that when her eyes are square she will make a wonderful stroke right into the center of the cup. This drill will keep your child focused and still over the putt.

Breaking Putts—Around the Tees

Stick a number of tees into the green at points that follow the break of the putt into the hole. The tees will help your child to see the curve as it breaks toward the hole. You may wish to use pennies or dimes in the same manner. I like to have a tee out to the left or right of the hole where the child needs to aim the putter and start the ball. When you work with this drill, it will really help the child to see and feel the amount of break he or she needs to play.

On the Green

If your youngster is around three, four, or five years old, place the ball one inch from the cup and let her tap it in. Then back up three to six inches and let her try again. Once she's fairly consistent from inside a foot, let her try two- and three-footers.

Older youngsters will enjoy putts that break—move with the curvature of the green. In a sense, putting on a slanted green is an art form, with balls taking parabolic routes to the cup. Where to hit the putt and how hard to hit the ball are highly instinctive. Practice is the key here.

Teaching pro Bobby McIver takes his young students out to the putting green and places a six-foot-long two-by-four to the hole. He places a ball right next to the wood and brings out a student. This trains the young player to look down the board and make sure his putting face is square; otherwise, the ball will never roll in. According to McIver, kids who make the perfect stroke but keep their blade open will miss every time.

"I tell the kids that if they can make six-foot putts, they can play anybody," says Bobby. "I have them practice until they can make ten in a row with the two-by-four, and then I take the board away. It's great practice."

When I played on the PGA Tour, I took my sweet time putting because I knew that putting accounts for 43 percent of a golfer's score. Jack Nicklaus was famous regarding his deliberations around the green, but he didn't have anything on me. I must have gone through thirty-seven checkpoints before drawing the flat stick back and rolling the ball toward the hole.

The human body is not wired to go through such a swing-thought "checklist," but I didn't know any better when I was playing on the tour. I took the "putt for dough" maxim to heart, and with thousands of dollars riding on each time I drew back my blade, I felt I deserved to take all the time I needed.

One time at the Las Vegas Open, I was paired with a close friend from Georgia—Lyn Lott. During our round, I must have driven him crazy as I stood over putts and kept looking up at the hole.

Stand over the ball.

Look up.

Stand over the ball.

Look up.

Stand over the ball.

Look up.

I was worrying about keeping my back low, tucking the right elbow in, leading with my hands, getting the right alignment, and not hitting too hard or too soft. When I finally stroked the putt, Lyn could tell I was wishing the ball into the cup.

After our round, Lyn called me over.

"Wally, I need to talk to you," he drawled.

"Sure, Lyn, what's up?"

"Son, I'm going to tell you something to help your game."

"What would that be?"

"Wally, when you putt, the ball is gonna do one of two things. It's either gonna go in the hole or not. It can't do anything else."

I felt as though he had imparted the wisdom of the Dead Sea Scrolls because though I'm embarrassed to admit it I had never thought of putting that way before.

The next day, instead of fidgeting and fussing over my putts, I stepped over the ball, set myself, and said to myself, "It's either going in, or it's not." Bang! Putts started dropping big-time. I finished the round with a 65, shot a final-round 67, and finished second in that PGA tournament.

The moral of the story is that you can't have a dozen swing thoughts when you putt, just as you can't have a dozen swing thoughts when you're standing on the tee. The mind goes on overload. Too much "reading" of the putt can make your child tense and fill his brain with too much conflicting information. The result is often an indecisive stroke, and indecisive putts are sure misses.

It's best to putt by feel, and feel comes from practice and studying the break on the greens. It's been said that a successful putter must have the ability to judge the slope, the sensitivity to feel the proper speed, and the courage to act on a decision once it has a been made. That's also a good metaphor for life, wouldn't you say?

It may sound like heresy for me to say this, but the biggest thing about putting for youngsters is *not* so much putting into the hole but knocking the putt the right length. Kids should learn to putt twelve to eighteen inches past the hole because a ball that never reaches the hole can never go in, right? I'll settle for kids learning to putt the ball within a two-foot circle of the hole, however. When kids (or adults) blow the ball five to ten feet past the hole and miss the "comebacker," they become frustrated with the game in a hurry.

As your youngsters improve, you'll want to implant the idea that putts have to at least *get* to the hole to have a chance to drop in. As that noted sage Yogi Berra once said, "Ninety percent of putts that are short don't go in."

Chipping

Now your children are ready to start chipping, which is defined as shots from near the green in which the ball rolls farther than it flies. Compare this shot to bowling. Have the kids stand by the side of the green, take a golf ball in their hand, and stride forward to place the ball on the green just over the edge. Then instruct them to roll the ball to the hole as in bowling. Explain to them that this is the objective in chipping, to get the ball on the green and let it roll all the way to the pin.

The distance of the shot will vary as to how far children take their clubs back. What is important is that children follow through, even on a short backswing. In other words, you do not want your children getting into the habit of taking a backswing and stopping the club once the ball is struck. If that happens, they will have to put the "brakes" on their swings just as they are striking the ball. Not good. Because chipping is a precision short shot with a ministroke, the children should choke down on the grip. Using a 6- or 7-iron is a good club to start with.

With chipping, the ball should be placed just opposite the rear toe. When kids set up this way, the club and their forward arm should form a straight line to the ball. If you look at them straight on, you should see that both arms and the club form a lowercase *y*. The key to good chipping is to never break the *y*. Explain to your young golfers that the club is an imaginary train. The grip is the engine of a train with the clubhead being the caboose. As they stroke and swing their arms back and through toward the ball, they should never jackknife the train. The leading hand pulls the club through so that the *y* stays intact throughout the stroke.

For chipping and pitching, have the kids imagine themselves as being a large grandfather clock. The club hangs down in front of them at the six-o'clock position. As they swing their arms and club backward away from the ball, the club will swing to seven, eight, and nine o'clock, going back and coming through past the six-o'clock position to five, four, and three o'clock.

When they imagine themselves as a clock, it will give them a good feeling for the distance that they need to swing the club and also for the amount of speed to strike the ball and send it the desired distances. Therefore, for the chip, the club should swing away to eight o'clock and through to four o'clock. Have fun with these creative chipping drills.

Pendulum Motion— Cross Handed

To feel how the forward hand needs to lead the way so there is no breakdown with the wrist, have your child chip balls with the hands reversed on the grip. Be sure she stands with the normal addressed position with her weight on the forward leg. This drill will help the child to develop the needed feeling of pulling the clubhead through the ball rather than hitting at it.

Path (Two-by-Fours)

The chipping stroke is a true pendulum motion, back and through just like a putt. In the picture, the student has placed two two-by-four pieces of wood in the direction of the cup approximately eight inches apart. Then as the child swings the club back and forth, the two-by-fours will keep the club from swinging around causing the face to open and close rather than staying square to the line. This will also help the student to feel how nice and tall they must stand in order to make a consistent chip. I like to have the kids imagine they are a general standing straight with his chest stuck out to show off his medals. When you use the two-by-fours, you will also find that the closer you move toward the ball the easier it is for the arms to swing back and forth in a pendulum motion. Some of the pros on the tour have the ball within six inches of their right toe in order to produce a consistent pendulum stroke.

Stance Stability—Crossed Legs

It is essential for good chipping to keep your weight on the front foot and not shift your weight to the back foot as you swing. In this drill take your normal stance and then bring your back foot in front of your left foot. Chip the ball on to the green. The "cross your legs" drill will help you remember to keep your weight on the left foot as you play all of your chip shots.

Distance and Direction— Landing Pad

Here is a drill that will save strokes and greatly improve your child's consistency by teaching him or her how far the ball rolls on the green. Stake out a one-foot square spot on the green and outline it with tees and string. Practice chipping to this "landing pad" until you consistently place your chips in the boxed area and roll the ball near the

hole. Go back and practice at different distances away from the green, with different clubs, to develop a feeling for the amount of carry the ball makes with those clubs as well as the amount of roll toward the hole. This drill builds a wonderful image for the kids to take on to the golf course when they actually play, but most of all it gives them a fun challenge to do when they are out practicing.

Fundamentals—Clotheslines

You can see in the picture below that I have stuck two reflectors into the fringe and strung surveyors tape from end to end, approximately one foot high. You may wish to use broken shafts and string or dowels for this drill. Practice chipping the ball below the tape and on to the green, enabling it to roll to the hole. This forces the children to play the ball farther back in their stance and to keep their hands moving forward throughout the stroke rather than scooping the ball. It is an excellent way to have fun as they learn how to mechanically play the correct chip shot.

Pitching

Pitching is similar to chipping because these shots are hit near the green, but with pitching the ball flies farther than it rolls. The swing is made with a pendulum stroke, as in chipping. The amount of arm swing depends on how far the ball should be struck. Most pitch shots are played by using a 9-iron or wedges. These clubs loft the ball into the air and will help to produce the desired height and distance of the shots needed. With a pitch shot, the ball should generally be placed in the middle of the stance. It is an arm swing like the chip shot, only as you get farther away from the green, a natural wrist set will be added. For the pitch shot, the swing is generally swung from nine o'clock to three o'clock. The key to pitch shots, as well as chip shots, is to eliminate any excessive body movement. The weight should be kept more on the front foot than on the back.

Explain to the kids that the pitch shot is very much like pitching a ball under-handed up on to the green. Have the kids do this before they play a shot with a golf club. Have them stand sideways in a golfer's stance with a ball in their rear hand and swing it back and forth, throwing it all the way on to the green and letting the ball trickle to the pin. This will give them an idea of how it is an arm swing, and that the amount of arm swing determines the distance the ball will travel. An infinite num-ber of variables to pitch shots exist because they can be hit in so many ways.

Have fun with your children working on these different pitches. Use different clubs as you move far-ther away from the green and have them feel the distances by swinging their arms not hitting with their hands. Remember the illustration of an elephant swinging its truck. This is what they should feel when they hit the pitch shot.

Here are some helpful pitching practice exercises.

Distance—Bucket Drill

Pitching the ball on to the green and watching it roll to the flagstick is an important skill to have. The key to good pitches is landing the ball in the correct area on the green. After playing a few pitches, place a bucket or wastebasket on to the green where you want the ball to land. Then play some shots up in the air trying to land them in the bucket. Note where the balls roll after they hit the green. Adjust the bucket to where it is placed on the green the proper distance. Then have some fun. This is one drill that you can practice in your backyard, either using golf balls or tennis balls. It is a great visual image to take out to the golf course.

Pendulum Swing—Big Sponge

In pitching you want to have a total pendulum motion created with the forearm swinging back and forth. The hands simply ride along on the club as it swings. To gain that feeling, take a large automotive figure-eight sponge and place it between the child's forearms. Then swing the club back and through, hitting shots on to the green. It is challenging, but it will help the child feel how the arms swing back and through together. If the sponge falls out, then he is not making the correct stroke. This is great for developing the tempo and the needed "oomph" for getting the ball up on to the green.

Swing Motion—Broom

Using a household broom to gain the sweeping feeling is critical for pitches. In the picture, notice that I am mimicking the correct swing behind my student.

Have your child do some broom sweeps, imagining that he is playing a pitch shot up to the green. Have him brush the grass on the way back and on the way through, feeling the motion. Then have him pick up a club and brush some balls up on to the green using the same motion.

Sand

Sand play is a more advanced shot for the beginning junior golfer. The sand wedge is designed to help explode the ball out of the sand trap and on to the green. It is the only shot in golf in which you intentionally try to miss the ball. The sand wedge has a very wide and heavy base to the club. When the club enters the sand behind the ball, it will naturally push the sand into the ball, lofting it on to the green. With most sand shots, you want to play the ball slightly forward of center and have the club enter the sand approximately one to two inches behind the ball. The key with the sand shot is to keep the clubhead swinging through the sand and underneath the ball. The sand shot is generally swung from nine o'clock to three o'clock.

One way to help kids feel this shot is to tee up a ball in the sand, pushing the tee down until the top of it is level with the sand. Then, as the kids swing the club back and through, have them swing through the sand under the ball and try to hit the middle of the tee, with the leading edge of the club throwing the tee out on to the green. When their focus is below the ball, the ball will flow out on a bed of sand on to the green. It is a great way to work with the kids. Remember, let the club do the work. The focus is not on hitting the ball but moving the sand up on to the green.

The following are some fun sand exercises that you can do with the kids. Again, remember to participate when you all go out to practice.

Moving Sand—Blocks of Wood

I found that most kids shift their focus to the ball rather than the sand. To have them be more sand oriented, take some blocks of wood or little plastic toys and toss them into a sand trap. Circle around each of them with your finger, and then have the child attempt to blast the small-circled island of sand and the wood block or toy on to the green. Then place balls on some islands of sand and have them imagine that the balls are the blocks of wood. They will have some fun with this one.

Acceleration—Two Balls

To develop a feeling of how much sand to take with sand shots, have the child place two balls next to each other lined up toward the putting surface. Then have her try to blast both balls out on to the green. This drill helps the child move the clubhead consistently through and under both of the balls. If you can get two balls out of the bunker consistently, one ball will be a piece of cake.

Sand Movement—Footprint

Have your child make a shallow footprint in the direction of the pin. Then have him practice swinging gently and completely, erasing the footprint using the bottom of the club. Then place a ball in the middle of the footprint and have him still erase the footprint. When the focus is not on hitting the ball but moving the sand, the ball will come out quite naturally as the club does its work.

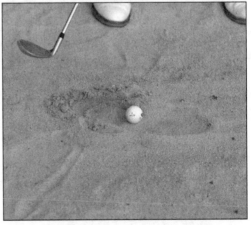

Angle of Attack—Colored Tape

To help your child feel the amount of sand to take as well as the action of the clubhead moving through on a descending *and* accelerating splash, place two pieces of colored tape about a foot apart. Set the ball about three inches behind the front tape and have your child swing away. The goal is to miss the rear tape, cut under the ball, and pick up the forward tape, splashing the ball on to the green.

This drill enables the child to feel the correct angle of attack and acceleration through the ball rather than trying to scoop the ball up on to the green. If there is a scooping action, they will more than likely hit the first tape and fail to get the ball out of the trap.

The Long Game

We are not referring here to booming drives off the tee but to the long iron shots to the green. For youngsters, that probably means 100 yards or more; for adults, 150 yards or more. Fine shots here can lower scores in a hurry—even turn four strokes into two. Awry shots land a player "in jail" and carry heavy penalties. You never want to hear what ABC's Jim McKay said during the Pebble Beach National Pro-Am tournament regarding a famous Hollywood actor: "Now here's Jack Lemmon, about to play his all-important eighth shot."

While you're seeking distance off the tee boxes, long iron shots call for accuracy—if you have an iron or 5-wood in your bag that can reach the green. Selecting the right iron is vital. Your child will have to learn which club to pull from the bag when he is 110 yards out, 120 yards, 130 yards, and so forth

Teach him to look for yardage markers on the course. Many courses have 200, 150, and 100 markers in blue, white, and red "hubcaps" in the middle of the fairway. Others have markers along the side of the fairways; yardage counts can also be found on sprinkler heads. Keep in mind that these yardage counts are for shots to the middle of the green, so if the pin is tucked way in the back of the green, better add a club. If the green is elevated, add a club. If you are hitting from a fairway bunker, add two clubs.

The best way to practice the irons is to start one hundred yards from the green and hit several dozen balls. Then move back ten yards and try the next club. As the distance increases, you will become better acquainted with how far you hit each club.

From one hundred yards out, your children want to be making a power circle swing—the full swing. I think it's important for kids to get used to taking a regular cut at the ball.

"There is something about practice at golf, about the steady self-discipline of playing shot after shot with the same club at the same objective, that gives strength to the soul."
—P. G. WODEHOUSE

11

IS THERE A PRO
IN THE HOUSE?

*Y*ou'd think with all the high-tech advancements in the game—oversized clubheads, bubble-shafted clubs, baffler woods, square-groove irons, perimeter-weighted tungsten balls, spikeless shoes, electric carts, manicured tee boxes, close-cropped fairways, laser range finders, and carpetlike greens—that the golf game of the average American would improve.

Yet handicap averages are *not* going down, according to the United States Golf Association, which tracks such things. We're buying expensive titanium-juiced clubs, but we're not posting better scores. We're peering through laser range finders, but our approach shots aren't finding the green.

Perhaps the problem is the person looking at you in the mirror. But no one wants to hear that. Nor does the public want to know they're playing golf as badly as ever, even with the technological advancements. That attitude doesn't surprise me, seeing as only 5 percent of the golfing public has ever taken a lesson. On the other hand, it seems like 95 percent of the John Q. Golfers of the world have run down to Joe Bob's Golf Mart and maxed out their credit cards to cart home the latest set of high-tech drivers and irons.

This trend tells me that we are a fickle audience in search of the quick fix. We really don't want to *work* at getting better; we'd rather purchase an expensive driver and let 'er rip. We may gain twenty yards with the new Technoblast DDP driver, but more likely we're going to slice the ball deeper into the woods.

Here's how too many golfers think today:

- *I want to be told how to do it, but I don't want to work at it.*
- *Just give me a club; I don't have time to practice. And when I practice, I want to practice what I like to hit, and I like hitting my driver.*

I see guys out on the range, swinging out of their shoes and trying to airmail the ball past the 250-yard marker. They have an oversized driver in their hands, and they love watching the ball go a long way. But do they practice their chipping game or short irons? No, because delicate chips don't have the same *thwack*. Too many adults fail to analyze their games and what they could do to improve their score. They go out on the course and get frustrated and angry and don't understand why their scores don't improve. The answer is that they are spending all their time on their long game and no time on their chipping.

David Duval, who won the British Open in 2001, had a father who made him chip a shag bag of balls with just his left arm before he could go to the practice tee. To his credit, David accepted this advice from his father, and he's done well by it. The next time you stroll by a driving range, count the people working on their short game.

Of course, the pendulum can swing the other way. Some people can be so wrapped up in reading instructional books, taking lessons, and fiddling with their swings that they become *overcoached*. Gary Player, a former Masters winner, said, "No matter how many lessons and bits of advice you receive from coaches, you still have to play with a certain amount of instinct."

I agree, and you—and your children—will develop that instinct through practice and through trying different shots from different lies. Practicing from the driving mat must be supplemented with chipping around the practice green.

One of the benefits I hope will come from *The First Tee Shot* is that this book will also help *you* build a better game for yourself as you infect your kids with the golf bug. In terms of learning a better swing, this book is a double-edged sword that cuts both ways for you and your sons and daughters. There is no reason why your strapping teen can't hold a hula hoop over *your* shoulders while you learn the basics of a circular swing. I guarantee that if you follow the principles in this book, your game will improve markedly and your children will learn golf the right way.

Checking It Out

Now that I have you convinced that you can benefit from lessons, let's talk about where professional instruction fits in with your kids. First of all, I'm all for golf lessons (which is what you'd expect to hear from someone who makes his living from teaching others how to play the game). Nonetheless, I recognize that there are parents who will not be able to do any of the aforementioned golf drills with their kids for myriad reasons. You may be busy dads or single-parent moms who simply do not have the time. You may find the task too daunting, or you know that you lack the requisite patience. As you pick your battles with your kids, you've discovered that golf is one war zone you want to avoid.

I'm fine with that. You know your children far better than I ever will, and you have a sixth sense of what works and what doesn't. At the same time, *someone* will have to show your children the rudiments of the game and how to swing a club correctly, and that is best done through a respected teaching professional. Moms and dads can become overbearing, too hands-on, and too involved; so unless money is an issue, send them to an expert as soon as you can.

If you believe it's time to seek professional instruction, here's what to do:

• *Start professional lessons between the ages of eight and twelve.* There are always exceptions, but generally speaking, most kids lack the motor skills for responding to golf instruction until they are in the third or fourth grades.

• *Determine whether or not your children want golf lessons.* Kids must have some degree of passion for the game, otherwise you're wasting your money. "If I have kids who show up two minutes before the lesson, haven't warmed up, then take the lesson and go straight home, then they are probably taking lessons because their parents want them to," top PGA teaching pro Charlie Sorrell said in an interview. "But if I see kids who come out early and hit balls and want to work at golf, then they have a desire to play."

• *Ask around.* Often the best way to find a good golf pro is to ask for a recommendation from golfing friends at school, business, or church. The pro's personality is the key. Does he like kids? How does she relate to them? I would rather send my kids to a kindhearted pro at a scruffy driving range than a big name

Taking Lessons with Cindy Reid

Cindy Reid is in charge of the teaching program at TPC at Sawgrass Club in Jacksonville, Florida, home of the Tournament Players Championships every March.

Cindy, in her late thirties, is a teaching pro dynamo—but you'd have to be to head up the teaching program at such a prestigious course. Year-round, Cindy conducts clinics for executives from IBM, Anheuser-Busch, and American Express, but she also has a lesson book filled with appointments for dozens of juniors who want to learn from one of the best. Cindy teaches six days a week, and sometimes she can't say no on Mondays, her day off.

From her vantage point on the practice tee, Cindy has worked both with uninvolved parents and with parents who are *too* involved. As a parent of three grown children, I can appreciate how difficult it is for us parents to strike the right balance. Cindy can reinforce what the father is saying to his son or his daughter because the information is not coming "top-down" from father to child.

One time, Cindy was teaching a talented sixteen-year-old boy, and before the lesson, he and his father discussed what Cindy might say. The father told the son, "I think you're taking the club past parallel at the top," which meant that he was taking the club too far back.

"No, Dad, my swing is just fine. Let's see what Cindy says during the lesson."

The teenager hit a few warm-up balls for Cindy. After a half-dozen swings, she asked him to stop.

"Steven, when you get to the top of your swing, your club is going past parallel because your left arm is breaking down at the top. If you keep your left arm firmer at the top of your swing, you won't go past parallel as much."

"That's what my dad told me."

"I give you permission to listen to your father occasionally," Cindy laughed, as she winked at Steve's dad.

Cindy told me that this happens often, especially with teenage boys. "They don't want to be told things by their fathers," she said, "but I believe in reinforcing what parents are trying to do, but we all know it is a fine line between being overbearing and being supportive."

Cindy says parents should let their children decide whether to take lessons or not. When kids are playing golf for themselves—and not doing it because their parents want them to—then those kids are more likely to stay with golf after they leave home.

Because Cindy is female, I asked her about the benefits—and differences—between taking lessons from male or female pros. "I've seen many people take lessons from women because we have more patience," said Cindy. "This is not to say that great teaching pros like Jim Flick, Rick Smith, Dave Pells, and you, Wally, don't have much patience, because you wouldn't have gotten to where you are today without it. But with a female instructor, the patience level is high. We understand and relate to females well since we are also women. We speak in a softer voice. We can talk in terminology to women without belittling them or making them feel as though they don't know anything."

I asked Cindy if she teaches boys and men differently.

"Actually, I teach everybody the same," said Cindy. "It's just second nature for me. Golf is golf."

attached to a semiprivate course. Don't forget that many head pros don't want to be bothered giving junior lessons, so they slough off the junior program to their less-skilled, less-experienced assistants. Find out who does the actual hands-on instruction.

• *Evaluate the facility.* Are the grounds kept up? Are the synthetic mats in good shape? Do they play with quality range balls, or are all the balls nicked and lopsided? Is there an adequate practice area for pitching, chipping, putting, and bunker practice? The state of the golfing facility says a lot for the vibrancy of the junior golf program.

• *Look for a PGA or LPGA member.* Both associations have stringent qualifications for becoming a teaching professional; it's like the Good Housekeeping seal of approval. Male versus female pro? Equal opportunity reigns here, although women are more nurturing than men, which might be an important consideration for the reluctant golfer in your family.

Although this is not a make-or-break issue, I would try to find an instructor that shares your Christian worldview. As kids reach their teens years, they have a tendency to stop listening to Mom and Dad and hear only from their peers and other authority figures in their lives. A kind, friendly coach who can impart godly wisdom while straightening out a swing is the best of both worlds, if you ask me.

• *Evaluate the pro's teaching style.* My complaint with most golf instruction is that it's *way* too technical. If the pro spends most of the lesson talking theory while the kids are standing around, chances are your youngsters will become bored stiff. The most important point of this book is this: Kids learn better when they are *shown* how to hit the ball, not *told* how to hit it. I believe 85 percent of all learning is visual, which is why I always demonstrate first and then talk about what happened. Kids relate to visual aids, and those pictures stay longer in their minds.

Someday I would like to conduct a clinic without saying a word—and become the Marcel Marceau (the famous French pantomimist) of golf teaching. Seriously, if I had to, I could give an hour lesson without saying a word, using only pantomime and training aids. Kids learn by imitation, so give them something to imitate. That's why I highly recommend instructors who use training aids.

• *Have your kids invite a friend.* Your youngsters will feel more comfortable if they bring along a buddy to their lesson. I also recommend group lessons at the beginning because it's cheaper.

• *Be aware of the student-teacher ratio.* How many students does the instructor have during a group lesson? I say eight to ten is the maximum; any more, and your child will receive little hands-on attention. Four-to-one is a superb ratio.

• *Ask if video is used.* Since kids learn by seeing and learn by imitation, a junior golf program with access to video playback has a great teaching tool in their hands.

• *Decide between half-hour versus one-hour lessons.* If it's a group lesson, make it an hour (unless you have children under eight; then thirty minutes is plenty). As for private lessons, I would start with a half hour because pros generally cannot keep children interested longer. You can always go to an hour if your older child can hold his concentration for sixty minutes, or if he is enamored by golf and starting to improve quickly.

• *Determine frequency of lessons.* Parents, you'll like this advice: most pros I've talked with believe that one hour a month is sufficient. Any more, and pros can boggle your children's young minds with too many mechanics. Depending on the age and maturity of your youngster, some kids can handle a greater lesson load. Cindy Reid, teaching professional at the TPC at Sawgrass golf course (see p. 116), says a Texas family flies to Florida twice a year to take three days of golf lessons with her. The children—fifteen, thirteen, and twelve—love golf, and their parents obviously have the financial resources to pay for expensive lessons and travel to get there. "But you know what?" says Cindy. "These parents have been so positive with their kids from the day they started."

• *Watch a lesson.* Adults are usually welcome to watch from a comfortable distance as long as they don't interfere with the lesson. Is the pro engaged? Are her drills worthwhile? If the kids are practicing 8-iron chips from just off the green without any instruction, then you are wasting your money because that's something you could do with your children.

• *Check out your child's attitude.* How is she feeling? Overwhelmed? Too competitive? How's her group? If your child is a fast learner but she's stuck with bored kids, she could get turned off. On the flip side, if she's at the bottom of her class and the other kids are doing better, she may push her exit button.

• *Weigh private lessons.* No doubt that private lessons are costly, ranging anywhere from twenty-five to seventy-five dollars per hour. You can trim that cost by having your children take half-hour lessons or by having them split a sixty-minute lesson. An experienced pro should be able to give you good input about your children's game and recommend moving them into competitive golf. The step into competitive golf must not be taken lightly. Look for intermediate steps. Many clubs stage small events in which juniors play scrambles and best balls to keep the competition low-key.

• *Make a commitment to your instructor.* One shot of instruction won't hack it. You need to stick with a teaching pro for at least a series of lessons so she can get to know your children and their swings. At the same time, don't be afraid to change instructors if your children are getting nothing out of their lessons.

• *Find out about any follow-up.* Does the instructor prescribe "homework" between lessons? Does she present a written practice plan or give you a video to watch? Are there any written evaluations at the end of the series?

• *Ask whether kids receive a discount on range balls.* Some lesson programs include discounted range balls as an incentive to practice between lessons. Ask if such a plan is available.

Paying retail to hit golf balls at a driving range is not cheap. A "large bucket" contains around seventy balls and usually costs six dollars. A rapid-firing golfer can burn through a bucket in twenty minutes.

Teach your child to take his time on the range. Show him how to go through a routine—deciding where to hit the ball, checking out his stance, and practicing the circle swing a couple of times—before he hits.

I've seen too many kids (and adults, for that matter) hit ball after ball with no thought of what they want to accomplish on the practice tee. They are like "Iron Mikes," the mechanical machines that test clubs and balls. These kids scoop a ball onto the mat with their clubhead, waggle once, and fire away. Ball on the mat, waggle once, fire away. It does no good to practice the wrong routine over and over, especially when the results are terrible.

Have them take their time! A large bucket should last a half hour or longer if they go through a good swing routine prior to each shot. I can still hear my father's voice: "Now, Wally, practice doesn't make perfect. Perfect practice makes perfect."

Golf is a game that practically demands perseverance and patience. These are qualities found throughout the Bible, and you can remind your children how Joseph persevered after he was sold into slavery by his brothers, or how Jesus resisted temptation during forty days in a huge desert sand trap. Remind your children that they will not hit a perfect shot every time (or even very often), so they must persevere and realize that it takes time to get better and better. *Perfect practice makes perfect.*

Believe it or not, one of the more interesting aspects of a pro golf tournament is watching players such as Tiger Woods and David Toms warm up on the practice tee. Most tournaments erect stands behind the driving range because many fans enjoy watching their favorite pros loosen up. From the stands you can see the pros taking their sweet time between warm-up shots, thinking through their swings, and conceptualizing the type of shot they want to hit.

When I was on tour, I would start with my upper irons—7, 8, and 9—and get a feel for the ball and my swing before moving to the more difficult clubs. When I hit my woods, I would pick a spot—say the back corner of the range—and hit ball after ball toward the target. For my short game, I hit for pins placed on the range. But you can hit for anything, if you give yourself the goal. On rainy days, I've even seen pros aim for certain puddles on the driving range!

12

THE THROES OF COMPETITION

As someone who has stared down his share of knee-knocking six-foot putts for par at the Masters golf tournament, I can unequivocally make this statement: It was much more nerve-racking watching my son Scott play in a tournament or high school match than it ever was playing at Augusta National.

Parental nervousness is universal when sons and daughters strap on their carry bags and sign up for a competitive golf tournament, be it a low-key nine-holer on a scruffy par-3 course or the final round of a "major" before millions of TV viewers. I've stood next to pacing fathers and hand-wringing mothers at PGA Tour events while their sons were walking up the fairway of number 18, hoping to preserve a one-shot lead. They were experiencing the stuff of high drama.

If your children compete in junior golf tournaments, steady yourself for the highs and lows to come. One of my difficult moments came when Scott, seven or eight years old at the time, was playing in one of his first tournaments. In those days, parents could follow at a respectful distance as long as they didn't attempt to talk to their children. (Today, some junior tournaments do not allow parents to walk the course with their children because too many were coaching their kids or helping them cheat. I'll have more to say about this later.)

At this particular event, my wife, Debbie, and I could tell by Scott's body language that he was not a happy camper. He was struggling to keep his game together, and we felt for him with each awry swing. We found it difficult not to be able to even encourage him.

On a short par-3, Scott sailed his ball into a gaping trap guarding the pin. Scott's drive found the middle of a bunker with a huge lip that must have looked like a great wave about to crash. He gamely walked into the trap with his rake, set his feet, and took a swing. The ball smacked the lip and rolled back down to his feet. Another swing. The ball rolled to his feet. And another swing. And another. And another.

I wanted to shout out, "Scott, just knock the ball backward out of the bunker, then chip and take your putts," but I couldn't. Finally, on the ninth try, the ball miraculously bounced off the lip and onto the fringe. Scott chipped and two-putted for his 13.

As he stomped off the green, Scott shot a look at Debbie and me. "How come you never taught me that shot, Dad?" he grimaced.

I was speechless, which I was supposed to be, but I was also taken aback by his remark. I had given Scott plenty of sand lessons. What happened was that he had encountered an unusual situation (a very high lip on the bunker), panicked when he couldn't get out, and taken his frustrations out on me.

Kids will do that because of their immaturity, and it takes a steady father and mother to roll with the punches. Scott was experiencing the pressure of tournament golf. As Bobby Jones, the great player from the 1920s once said, "There are two kinds of golf: golf and tournament golf."

What Bobby Jones was saying is that tournament golf is played under the crucible of competition. Tournament golf can forge young golfers into par-toughened players or chase them away from the game. Golf is a subjective activity scored in an unforgiving manner. Golf is not a team sport, so it demands a different mental approach. You must be able to put bad shots behind you. If you don't, you'll go crazy on the golf course.

Tournament golf has a way of determining which kids thrive on competition, which kids are nonplused, and which kids can't rise to the occasion. Because of these aspects, I would emphasize the fun of the game more than the thrill of victory because there is going to be the "agony of defeat."

That is why I would be very careful about harboring dreams of your son walking up to number 18 at Augusta, doffing his cap as waves of applause shower him, or watching your daughter triumphantly raise the U.S. Open trophy above her head. The odds of them reaching the pinnacle of the sport are infinitesimal, barely worth discussing.

Just a couple of hundred Americans are making a decent living playing golf—out of 40 million players in this country. Granted, the household names and up-and-coming stars are taking home wheelbarrows full of cash, but all the money is stacked at the top. Those ranked after number two hundred aren't doing much

---

The Mental Side of the Game

I know, golf can be so mental that people go crazy playing it. If your children get into junior golf, they should adopt what Masters winner Fuzzy Zoeller once said about playing golf: "You hit it. Find it. Hit it again. Add 'em up."

Have your children read these foundational truths that will hopefully keep them safe and sane on the course:

1. *Don't worry about things you can't control.* That includes bounces, lies, course conditions, even who you're paired with.
2. *Your biggest weapon is your attitude.* Keep thinking positive thoughts. It's tough to do, but keep working at it.
3. *Do your best and don't worry about the rest.* Unless you are the second coming of Tiger Woods, there is always someone better than you and someone worse than you.
4. *Think perspective.* What's the difference between a birdie and bogey ten years from now? It's not the end of the world.
5. *Don't be afraid to step back.* If you're not committed when you start your swing, stop and regroup!
6. *Be best friends with yourself.* Self-hatred is a great destroyer.
7. *Focus on what you want to happen, not what* might *happen.* You often become what you think.
8. *Expect to get into trouble on the golf course.* You can face it head on.
9. *Replay good shots in your mind.* This will help you stay on track.
10. *Gamesmanship can come back and haunt you.* Learn to compliment others.

Mastering the art of playing well rests upon mastering the art of playing poorly. If you can accept imperfection and continue to play without fear, you will become a very good golfer.

more than breaking even after paying their expenses. The minor leagues of golf—the mini tours, the regional tournaments, etc.—are filled with hundreds of talented golfers chasing a pipe dream. Many are called, but few are chosen.

It's all right for your children to dream about qualifying for the U.S. Open, but temper those abstractions by helping them set short-range, medium-range, and long-range goals. Short-range goals would be breaking 100, making the school team, or placing in the top five in a junior tournament. Medium-range goals would be winning a local event or qualifying for an important regional competition. Long-range goals would be playing in college or in a national amateur event.

I'll tell you another thing: those with great talent often put it on display early. Harvey Penick, a famous teaching pro, once said he was walking by the first tee at Pinehurst when he heard a rifle shot go off. He looked up in time to see a young Sam Snead watching the flight of a tremendous drive. Sam Snead was good early, and he enjoyed an illustrious pro career in the 1940s and 1950s.

But even youthful prodigies who display a genius for the game are no sure bet. For every story like Tiger Woods, there are dozens more like Beverly Klass. Before she was four years old, Beverly's father introduced her to golf and believed she had been blessed with a special talent. In the National Pee Wee Championship, eight-year-old Beverly dusted the competition by sixty-five strokes! In 1967, at the tender age of ten, Beverly played her first LPGA pro event (the women's tour did not have a minimum age requirement at the time).

Some called Beverly the future of women's golf, but she became such a troubled adolescent that her parents committed her to a mental institution. When Beverly attempted a comeback at age twenty, she could no longer compete and quickly faded from the golf scene.

Questions to Ask

How do you feel about tournament golf? Are you ready for the entry fees and the carpooling and the long days? With a right attitude from you and your children, junior golf tournaments can be an excellent way for your kids to learn how to play the game, improve their scores, and continue the tradition of "fair play" that has been golf's calling card for more than one hundred years. Tournament play can provide more of those mentoring moments that bring a father and a mother closer to their children.

Many major cities have junior golf associations that promote the sport and organize tournaments for novice, intermediate, and advanced players. The tournament fees are usually very modest. The San Diego Junior Golf Association, for instance, stages tournaments at some of San Diego's finest courses—ones that most juniors would never get to play—and charge just ten to fifteen dollars per tournament round. And the juniors get a free hot dog and Coke after posting their scores.

Checklist

If you're going to dive into junior golf, keep these things in mind:

• *Be a good role model on the course.* Do you slam your irons into the fairway after hitting a banana slice into the adjoining fairway? What does your body language say after you four-putt?

You may not think so, but your kids are soaking in the way you comport yourself on the golf course. Let them see that your mood or demeanor doesn't dramatically change with how well or how poorly struck your shot was. Let them see you as a fun-loving father or mother who's full of encouraging words.

• *Don't force tournament golf down their throats.* Not every child *wants* to play tournaments. A good indication that she does is when she asks you whether she can enter a tournament. Otherwise, play it cool. Sure, you can ask whether she wants to enter the local Rotary Club junior tourney, but be sure to gauge her response as an indication of her interest. Is it strong or tepid?

• *What's their attitude and aptitude for the game?* If your youngster loves to stay out until dark on the chipping green, or has been blessed with a burning desire to practice, those would be good indications that your son or daughter wants to be competitive. But if it is always *your* idea to play golf, maybe it's time to lower expectations.

• *If possible, have your children play the course before the tournament.* Your children will feel much more comfortable playing the course the second or third time around. Golf courses have a way of "ganging up" on players, with one tough hole after another. If the course proves to be the reincarnation of San Francisco's Olympic course, at least your child will be mentally prepared for an arduous outing. Playing a course in advance of a tournament will also help your youngster attain an appreciation for the speed of the greens.

• *Play practice rounds as "real" rounds.* If you're playing a pretournament round together, you might say something like this on the first tee: "Jeremy, you have your first tournament coming up next weekend, and you're going to have to get used to playing without any mulligans or takeovers. I just want you to know that we won't be taking any mulligans, even on the first tee. This will be good practice for the tournament." The sooner kids learn that every shot counts, the better.

• *Ask yourself: Is my son (or daughter) "wired" for competition?* If your child is competitive, wants to participate in junior tournaments, and is practicing enough to make the investment worthwhile, go for it. You will have to look for cues to determine how your child is bent.

Blake played a couple of tournaments before he was ten years old, and I caddied for him, which was a blast. He talked to everyone—me, his playing partners, the marshal, and the rules official—as we strode down the fairway. I don't think he knew what he was shooting. He just didn't care.

This did not surprise me because Blake had given me clues that he was a free-spirited individual. One time when he was in the first grade, his school sponsored a track-and-field day. He and a half-dozen classmates entered

What Dad Did Right
BY SCOTT ARMSTRONG

I broke 80 before I was twelve years old, but Dad never made me play tournaments. In those preteen and early-teen years, I was more interested in team sports such as baseball, so Dad let me play Little League and Pony League baseball.

In fact, I didn't play much competitive golf until my freshman year of high school at Orangewood Christian School in Orlando. I was the number-one player, and our little school had a great golf team. We even took the state title in my senior year.

Dad left it up to me whether I wanted to play more junior golf tournaments. Looking back, I wish I had entered more tournaments because competition takes your game to a whole new level. I think I would have become a strong player. But it was my decision, and Dad allowed me to make it.

the one-hundred-yard dash. Blake burst out of the blocks way ahead of everyone else. About ten yards short of the finish line, he saw me cheering him on.

He stopped running. "Hi, Dad," he waved. "How's it going?"

"Run, Blake, run!"

"Why?"

All the boys passed him like he was standing still—because he *was* standing still.

• *Let them hit balls before they start.* Would you expect Roger Clemens to walk out to the mound and start firing away without warming up? There can't be worse feelings in sports than standing on the number 1 tee in front of everyone waiting to play, and cold-topping your drive thirty yards to the right. Have your children hit balls at the course, or if that is not possible, drop by a driving range along the way. The same goes for putting. They have to putt for at least five to ten minutes before teeing off.

• *Realize that you may not be able to walk the course with them.* The trend in junior golf, as I mentioned before, is that you will not be allowed to follow your children as they play—all because some undisciplined and unscrupulous parents ruined it for everyone else. Your only chance to see them play will be off the first tee and the finishing green.

If you live in a region of the country where you *can* follow your children, take advantage of it. Trailing your children will be a treat, although spectators are asked to stay on the cart path or in the rough areas. Be sure to remain a reasonable distance away (twenty yards is recommended) and never give any advice on club selection or how a putt breaks. This could result in a two-stroke penalty! Nor can you give rulings on the Rules of Golf. In stroke play, when a player is in doubt regarding a rules situation, he can play two balls and report the facts to the Rules Committee before handing in his scorecard.

• *Become their caddy.* Some tournaments will let you caddy for you son or daughter, and if I were you, I would jump all over that opportunity. The chance to be on your child's bag (as they say in caddy lingo) means that you get to be friend, counselor, and coach all in the same day. But you can't be a "parent," if you catch my drift. You want to follow the three rules of being a good caddy:

1. You show up.
2. You keep up.
3. You shut up.

• *Talk about cheating.* Radio commentator Paul Harvey once joked, "Golf is a game in which you yell 'fore,' shoot six, and write down five." While it may be amusing to joke about, more and more golfers are indeed writing 5's on their cards when they should be penciling in a 6 or 7—especially in tournaments. It's probably the day and age we live in, but I've heard of more and more accounts of kids (and adults) cheating in tournament play.

Some may want to play so well that they succumb to the pressure to count fewer strokes, kick the ball out of a hazard, or improve their lie in the rough. Tell your kids that if they ever cheat—and get caught—they might as well put a sign on their back that says "Cheater" for a long time. That's a terrible albatross to wear around one's neck, and it will probably drive them from the game.

Golf is an honorable game in which participants are expected to self-police themselves, but as TV golf commentator Dave Hill said, "Golf is the hardest game in the world to play and the easiest to cheat at." For some people, the temptation is too great, but if you can encourage your youngsters to do the right thing because that is what God would have us to do, they will learn a lesson that they can apply elsewhere in their lives. Proverbs 11:1 says, "The Lord hates cheating, but he delights in honesty" (NLT).

• *After talking about cheating, talk about gamesmanship.* What's gamesmanship? It's winning by dubious or unsportsmanlike methods that do not actually break the rules.

Here's an example. Claude Harmon, a top-notch PGA pro from the 1950s and 1960s, was watching his sons play against each other in a big national amateur tournament. The format was match play, and Dick Harmon was beating his brother, Craig. In the middle of the back nine, Craig went into a slowdown mode—waggling extra long on the tee, taking his sweet time determining yardage on approach shots, and looking over putts from every conceivable angle. Craig did it to drive his brother crazy—and get him off his game.

Their famous father, who was in the galley, knew his sons well. "Stop these slowdown tactics and play golf!" he yelled out at Craig.

What are other ways to disrupt your opponent? Some golfers will stay in a person's line of sight and then move during the backswing. Others will bring a closed hand to their mouths and cough just as a putt is struck. Others will drop a club or pull the Velcro on the golf glove at critical moments. Such chicanery has no place in the game.

• *Give them a goal to shoot for.* Too much emphasis is placed on the scorecard total. Set realistic goals by encouraging your children to shoot for one par per each nine holes, or no triple bogeys, or all two-putts. The final score will take care of itself.

Matt Kuchar, one of the young guns on the PGA Tour (you'll learn more about Matt in the next chapter), says his Christian faith helps with the hard times and the good times of being inside the ropes. "Golf is like life," he said in an interview. "You get some good breaks and some bad breaks. It's how you handle it that makes the difference. My faith is a backbone for me, which is why I ask God to help me continually. I say a little prayer before each round, asking God to allow me to play to the best of my ability, and that I act like a gentleman and try not to let anything get to me."

• *Give them a great memory verse.* Take it from someone whose hands shivered standing on the first tee at Augusta: tournament golf causes weird physiological things to happen. If the hands aren't shaking, then the knees are knocking like a break-dancer. The pressure on your chest feels like someone sitting on you.

A great calming verse of Scripture is Philippians 4:13: "I am able to do all things through Him who strengthens me" (HCSB). It's a short verse that your youngsters can—and should—commit to memory. Remind them to whisper the verse to themselves when the heat is on and the pressure is mounting. Christ gives us strength when we do everything through him.

• *Expect the worst, hope for the best.* If your youngster has been barely breaking 50 for nine holes, don't expect that score to stand up under the hot glare of competition. I would expect something between 50 and 60, unless your child is the reincarnation of Jack Nicklaus.

• *When they come off the eighteenth green, don't ask what they shot.* You'll find out soon enough. Instead, you should ask, "How was it out there? Did you have fun? Do you want to get something to drink and tell me about your round?" Kids are often most talkative right after the event, so don't let that opportunity pass by. This would be a great time to take them out for an ice cream.

• *Watch your body language.* Remain impassive. Don't act too excited if your youngster scores well. Don't let your face fall and shoulders sag if he blew a tap-in putt. Give your child a hug or pat on the back, no matter what the result.

An Indelible Mark

If you log on to the Ladies Professional Golf Association (LPGA) Web site at www.lpga.com, check out the player profiles. Approximately 250 players were asked to name who they considered to be the major influence on their careers. Here are the results of the survey:

- 25 percent named their fathers
- 3 percent named their mothers
- 30 percent named both parents

In other words, close to 60 percent of the world's top women golfers said they were influenced most by their parents—particularly their fathers. One of the best-known father-daughter relationships is between Nancy Lopez—a U.S. Open winner and future LPGA Hall of Famer—and her father, Domingo. This Hispanic family lived in Rosewall, New Mexico—not exactly the golfing crossroads of the world—but Domingo was the parent who sawed off a 4-wood and placed it into the hands of his seven-year-old daughter, Nancy.

He taught her the rudiments of the game at the town's municipal course, and when Nancy started competing and beating everyone in sight, Domingo worked overtime at his auto body repair shop to pay for lessons and travel. Nancy's mother, Marina, gave up the game because she believed the family couldn't afford three golfers.

Domingo taught his daughter to "play happy" and to shrug off disappointing rounds. "My dad never got mad at me for playing badly; he just always said something to make me feel better," Nancy said.

In a *Golf* magazine article, sports psychologist Deborah Graham, who works with male and female pros, said that a parent's ability to separate a child's worth from his or her athletic performance is one of the keys to raising an emotionally healthy athlete.

"What makes all the difference is that the love for the game is not tied to the love for the child," said Debbie Graham.

• *Stay on the positives; don't dwell on the negatives.* Your child will make mistakes on the golf course—tons of them. To dwell on them is a sure turnoff. You want to feed your children heaps of praise, such as:

"That was a great approach shot coming in 18."

"You one-putted number 12? Way to go!"

"Sounds like you hit a really good shot. Tell me more about that."

Cindy Reid, who teaches at the TPC at Sawgrass, says when kids start reliving poor shots with you, change the subject. Here's how you can do it:

Peter: "I played so bad today, Dad."

Dad: "Bad?"

Peter: "I had an 8 on number 14. That's the long par-5."

Dad: "That's all right. Tell me about some of your good holes."

Peter: "There weren't any."

Dad: "There weren't any? OK, then tell me about some of your good shots."

Peter: "You know the short par-3 on number 8? I got it on the green, but it wasn't close enough for a birdie try."

Dad: "Did you two-putt?"

Peter: "Yes."

Dad: "Well, that was a good hole for you. You got your par. Were there any other good shots?"

Peter: "I drove well on number 1 and number 2."

Dad: "You mean you hit a good drive with everyone watching you on the first tee?"

Peter: "Yes."

Dad: "That had to feel good."

Peter: "But then I bogeyed the hole."

Dad: "So? It's tough getting off the first tee with everyone watching you."

Peter: "I suppose you're right. But on number 3, I put my ball into the lake."

Dad: "Yes, but how did you play the other two par-3s?"

Peter: "One par and one bogey."

Dad: "So you see, you didn't play them too bad."

Notice what Dad was doing? He was trying to get Peter off the negative shots and start talking about the good shots. Remind your youngster that everyone, no matter what their level, will hit poor shots during a round of golf. It's the next shot that counts.

• *Don't let golf dominate dinner table conversation.* Sure, you want to "talk out" or debrief following a tournament round, but be sensitive to the rest of the family, especially if you are all sitting around the dinner table. Believe it or not, there is more to life than golf. If Dad and Son #1 spend most of mealtime discussing the relative merits of 2-irons versus 5-woods, the younger children (and Mom) will tune out. They could develop a distaste for golf because they are not involved. Be sensitive in this area.

• *Keep a little perspective, please.* Dave Marr, a TV golf analyst, once said, "There are one billion Chinese, and they don't know about golf and they don't care about it."

Here's how my friend Bobby McIver taught perspective to a junior player who came off the course swearing a blue streak, tossing his bag to and fro, and generally announcing to anyone within earshot that golf was a lousy game and he was sick of it.

The kid had become a good player, but after that outburst, Bobby walked up to him and said, "Erik, we're going to go for a little drive."

"Where are we going?" asked the teenage player.

"We're going to Children's Hospital to visit a few kids with cancer."

The walk through the cancer ward shocked the young golfer. After realizing how fortunate he was to have the opportunity just to play golf, the boy never acted up on the course again.

"Play because you love the game,
not because you think you can make a lot of money.
If you play because you love it, everything will fall into place."
—WAYNE GRETZKY
HOCKEY GREAT AND GOLFER WITH AN 8-HANDICAP

13

"KOOCH" IS COOL

As a father, life doesn't get much better than this, Peter Kuchar thought to himself as he and his son, Matt, strode toward the treacherous eighteenth green at San Francisco's Olympic Club during the final round of the 1998 U.S. Open golf championship.

Peter had been on Matt's bag all week, but it never felt lighter as the twenty thousand fans stood and applauded *pere et fils* Kuchar as they approached the final hole of golf's most prestigious tournament, the U.S. Open.

Peter Kuchar won't forget June 21, 1998, for a long time because of the harmonic convergence of Matt's twentieth birthday and Father's Day. All day long, the massive galleries sensed something special as well, and they serenaded Matt with choruses of "Happy Birthday" and yelled "Happy Father's Day" to the beaming pop.

"It seemed like every hole I had a birthday song sung to me," said Matt. "It was the most memorable birthday I had." Prior to teeing off before the final round, the Olympic Club presented Matt with a big white-frosting cake.

Five hours later, this father-and-son duo walked up the eighteenth fairway as applause rained down on them. There was still some work to do. Matt needed to two-putt the eighteenth green to secure a top-15 finish, which would automatically qualify him for the 1999 U.S. Open. Olympic's eighteenth green was a slanted, nasty piece of real estate and a graveyard for those with two-putts on their minds.

Peter sidled up to Matt and handed him his putter. Peter saw his role as Chief Encourager and Head Cheerleader, not Dominating Dad who pulled the puppet strings of his golfing progeny. "We need this two-putt," Peter whispered. "Good luck."

Matt's approach shot had rested pin-high, leaving him with a twelve-foot curvy sidehill putt loaded with mischief. Matt studied the break and went through his routine, scanning the putting surface from behind and in front of the ball. Thinking birdie all the way, he rolled the rock toward the cup—but too aggressively. The ball slid by and embarked on a downhill trip that ended considerably further from the cup than its original starting point. Now Matt was left with twenty feet of green to negotiate for his par.

Many fathers would have rolled their eyes and let their body language say, *You dunce! Why didn't you just lag it for a tap-in?*

Instead, Peter remained impassive and allowed Matt to regather himself for his comebacker. Make it, and Matt would be invited back to the U.S. Open. Miss it, and he would be relegated to regional qualifying or some other mode of qualification.

Matt hitched his pants, took his time, and drilled the twenty-footer—icing on the cake of a memorable day. His final round score of 74 tied him for fourteenth place.

Afterward, Peter told reporters, "It's hard to believe that twenty years ago this kid was born. If the next twenty years are anything like this, it's going to be quite a ride."

I can't wait to see what kind of ride that will be. Matt earned his PGA card during the 2001 season, and I'm confident that he'll have a great career. Perhaps that's because I've known Matt ever since he and my son, Scott, played together on the Orangewood Christian School golf team in Orlando.

To gain a father-son perspective on their golf relationship, I interviewed Peter for *The First Tee Shot.* Here is a record of our interchange:

Wally: How did you get Matt into golf? A lot of parents are wondering what you did.

Peter: Matt had always been my little shadow from day one, but our story really begins when Matt was ten years old. At that time I was a tennis player, playing several times a week and competing in age-group tournaments. In 1988, I had a great year, winning the No. 1-ranking in Florida for players thirty-five and over. I said to myself, "That's it; you're not going to get any better, so it's time to take up something new."

For Christmas that year, my wife, Meg, upgraded our membership at the country club from tennis to golf, so I went out to the driving range and my shadow came with me. The difference between Matt and me was that he had a gift, and I didn't. I began putting the same effort in my golf game as I had in tennis. As we started playing golf together, I signed him up for a group clinic, and he learned all the right fundamentals, then used hard work and his athletics gifts to improve. Matt was truly a natural golfer from the first day he stepped foot on the golf course. His eye-hand coordination had always been exceptional.

Wally: Was there anything that you did to improve that hand-eye coordination?

Peter: Have you ever noticed that when you toss a ball to a little kid, he turns his head because he's afraid the ball might hurt him? As soon as Matt could basically stand up, I blew up balloons and tossed them toward him. Kids aren't afraid of balloons. After he learned to catch the balloons, Matt batted them with a plastic baseball bat, tennis racquet, whatever. When he was old enough, I started playing tennis with him, and by the time he was ten, he had won two state-sanctioned tournaments. We also played a lot of table tennis, which again helped his hand-eye coordination.

Throughout elementary school, I coached his soccer team, and he was always my best player. He was like a piece of clay that I could mold. It was quite a thrill to work with a child with that kind of ability.

Wally: Many kids won't let Dad work with them. What did you do to *not* be an overbearing father?

Peter: I made sports fun. When I coached soccer, I told the boys to dribble the ball—bounce it off their feet or their knees without letting the ball touch the ground. Then I would say, "Whoever can dribble the ball the most times gets a quarter." I went to practice with a lot of quarters, and I was happy to hand them out. Then I put them through relay and shooting drills, and whoever did the best got another quarter. They would play so hard for twenty-five cents. Those were some of the little things I did to make practice competitive yet fun.

I was cognizant when Matt and I started golf that I had to make it enjoyable for him. Consequently, I let Matt always drive the cart, not me, because that was fun.

Wally: You're a believer in rewards?

Peter: Yes, I am. Kids love having something to shoot for. I remember when Matt and I first started playing golf. I would give him a few strokes a hole, and then a stroke a hole, and then for about a week we were even. Then he just flew by me.

How Good Must You Be to Get a Golf Scholarship?

I put this question to Charlie Sorrell, a PGA Master Professional with a golf school located just outside Atlanta. Charlie has coached hundreds of junior golfers into collegiate golf, and 90 percent of his students earn some form of scholarship. Here's Charlie's breakdown for boys:

- If you want to play at a Division I school (Stanford, UCLA, University of Nevada at Las Vegas, University of Texas, Georgia Tech, University of South Carolina), then you must *average* 73 or better. For Division I schools where golf is not prominent, you should average 75.
- If you want to play at a Division II school (Fresno State, Ball State), then you must average between a 74 and 78.
- If you want to play at a Division III or NAIA school (in other words, small colleges that do not offer athletic

scholarships), then a 79 through high 80s scoring average should get you on the team.

For the girls, you can add a half-dozen strokes to those numbers, but as I mentioned before, there seem to be more opportunities for girls to earn golf scholarships these days. Even so, the bar is set fairly high if your son or daughter is to be awarded an athletic scholarship. One good point is that golf is an objective sport. How good a player you are is based on your scoring average, and that is a black-and-white statistic. You're named All-State or All-League based on what you shoot, not on the opinions of several coaches who saw you play.

Charlie says he tells his students, "If you're going to college to play golf, then you're going to college for the wrong reason. You need to get an education. If golf is part of it and you can be successful, then fine. But don't go to college just to play golf."

Wally: You've been caddying for your son in some of the PGA major tournaments the last couple of years. Many people, including myself, enjoyed watching the 1998 U.S. Open and all the fun you and Matt had out there. One of the most exciting moments was when Matt chipped in from off the green for a birdie, and you and the crowd got all excited. Some of the pros said you got *too* excited. Can you give us your side of the story?

Peter: During Friday's round, Matt was in deep trouble. He had hit his approach left of the green, leaving it on a little hill just off the putting surface. He had an uphill chip with no green to work with. He was definitely facing bogey or worse. But then he chipped in this delicate shot that bounced three times and dropped in the hole. The huge crowd went crazy, and I gave Matt a high five. The whole thing took five seconds.

Then it was defending U.S. Open champion Ernie Els' turn to putt. He had a long thirty-footer for birdie, a very difficult putt. But he snaked it in, and again the crowd went crazy. That left Justin Leonard to finish. He was facing a twenty-footer for birdie. He studied the putt and sent the ball shooting past the hole—way past. Then he missed an eight-foot comebacker. And another comebacker. Justin walked away from the fifteenth green with a four-putt, and he was steaming. The press made a big deal about it.

So let's see if we got this scenario down. Matt chips in, we high five. Ernie Els waits for the crowd to be quiet, then knocks in a thirty-footer for birdie. Justin then four-putts. Now whose fault is that? Justin, obviously, was very bothered by something or somebody, but why should it have been us?

Wally: What have been some other great moments carrying your son's bag in big tournaments?

Peter: I can name three. Matt's second shot on the seventeenth hole at the 1998 United States Amateur Championship, when he was two up with two holes to go, was just unbelievable. With all that pressure, he put his long approach to within six feet of the hole. Watching my son win the U.S. Amateur Championship was just a feeling you can't describe. Something like 6,666 golfers signed up to play, and to be the one left standing was just remarkable.

Then you have the 1998 Masters, where on Saturday Matt shot a 68 and was near the leader board. Walking up the eighteenth fairway with Matt on the final Sunday, with my son shooting the best amateur score in twenty years, was heaven on earth for a golfer.

Finally, caddying for him on Father's Day at the U.S. Open was a big highlight.

Wally: Do you have other children?

Peter: I have a daughter, Becky, also in her early twenties. She doesn't play golf, but she's an expert shopper. Seriously, she's a great young woman with talents in other areas.

Wally: How were you able to afford golf course fees, lessons, and tournaments?

Peter: It wasn't easy. I'm in the insurance business, and the good Lord has provided me and my family with a good income, but I was amazed to learn how expensive golf can be at the upper echelon.

Let me first start by saying there are grass-roots programs out there to get less-privileged kids introduced to the game of golf, and that's a good thing. I'm afraid, however, that having your son or daughter compete on a world-class amateur level is phenomenally expensive. When Matt was in high school, it was costing us ten thousand dollars a year for lessons, travel, and entry fees.

When Matt advanced beyond junior golf into amateur golf, it got to be a lot more expensive than that—maybe a little more than thirty thousand dollars per year. The sad part about that was that I had to pay for his expenses with after-tax money.

Wally: What do you mean by after-tax money?

Peter: Let me explain. When Phil Mickelson plays the British Open, he can deduct his airfare, his hotel, and his food because those are all business expenses for him. When Matt played the U.S. Open as an amateur, he couldn't deduct his airfare because he's an amateur, nor could he deduct his hotel, food, or other expenses. Was that fair? I don't think so. Was that the rule? Yes, that was the rule. So if it cost me thirty thousand dollars, how much did I have to earn to put thirty thousand dollars in my pocket? Well, the answer was fifty thousand dollars, of which twenty thousand dollars goes to taxes. That was not right, but those were the rules, and we played by the rules.

Wally: Very few parents have an extra fifty thousand dollars lying around in their budget. What do you say to them?

Peter: I certainly empathize with their plight. Because of the present-day rules we have, golf is becoming a game for the wealthy. That's what it has come to. You really need tons of dough to play this game on a world-class level, and I didn't have that kind of money, nor am I a wealthy guy. I know I have many people who would trade places with me, but that's the way it was. However, if you think I'm complaining for one second, you're wrong. Things worked out great for us.

Wally: Can't good junior golfers get help from their local golf association?

Peter: It depends on your region, but most golf association help stops when the junior turns sixteen years old. By the time Matt hit sixteen, we didn't get any more help.

Wally: Do you see the money situation as a fly in the ointment for junior golf in the future?

Peter: Yes, I do, but I guess you can get your feet wet and start out with local tournaments. Then if your kid does well, he advances to state and national tournaments, but that next level gets expensive. If your child is *really* good, you can always look at your golf expenses as prepaying his or her college tuition.

Wally: How many golf scholarships are there out there?

Peter: Let me tell you about the NCAA rules. If you're a Division I school, the maximum scholarships that can be granted are four and a half. I'm a Stetson

University graduate, which is Division I, but they give out only one scholarship. At Georgia Tech, where Matt went to school, they were much better endowed: the Yellow Jackets gave out four and a half full rides or equivalents. The University of Nevada at Las Vegas (UNLV), Oklahoma State, Clemson, Texas Christian (TCU)—all the elite schools—hand out four and a half rides. That's not very many, is it?

Wally: Well, you've got to be pretty darn good to get a full ride then.

Peter: That's exactly right. But the coach may decide to give three full rides and three partial scholarships.

Wally: How has golf deepened your relationship with Matt?

Peter: Seeing my son perform under the utmost pressure has been a tremendous experience for us. Sometimes when I watched him play, I couldn't even swallow because I was so nervous. Probably one of the best memories was during the first round of the Masters when Matt, as the U.S. Amateur champ, was paired with Tiger Woods. There must have been ten thousand on the first tee when they introduced both of them to tremendous applause. Standing at the first tee, I got this huge lump in my throat. I looked at my wife, Meg, and she had tears running down her cheeks.

Well, Matt teed it up and hit his driver 285 yards right down the middle. How he did that after that applause I'll never know, but that's what the great ones can do. I would have been lucky to just hit the ball.

Wally: Have you imagined what it will be like playing golf with your grandchildren?

Peter: Yes, and if they're Matt's kids, I guarantee you that I'll have the balloons blown up while they're still in the cradle. It'll be a real thrill to work with them. I'm not rushing it though. I'm enjoying life right now. I can tell him things that nobody else can because I'm his dad and his friend. I just know how to pump him up when the timing is right.

Wally: Give me an example of some type of encouragement.

Peter: At the U.S. Open, I remember walking up the eighteenth fairway with him on that Father's Day Sunday. I told him he was right on the bubble for finishing in the top fifteen, which was very important since the top fifteen are automatically invited to the U.S. Open the following year. Matt said, "Well, yeah, I'm going to birdie this hole."

We go to look at his ball, and he's got a twelve-footer on a very difficult green. Matt looked it over and then got real aggressive on his putt—the ball rolled twenty feet past the hole! But he drained that long putt to earn a return invitation.

Wally: Wait a minute. Did you say anything to him after he ran that first putt by the hole?

Peter: I couldn't say anything. He knew what he had done.

Wally: Why is golf such a great father-son game?

Peter: I guess it goes back to looking at every guy you watch on TV and hearing him say, "I learned from my dad." There's just something special about spending time with your son or daughter on a golf course. I can tell you this: my favorite foursome is my dad, my brother, and Matt. Few things in life are better than the four of us playing golf together.

Reminisces from Matt's First Coach

BY CHRIS BATEMAN

I wasn't the first person to show Matt Kuchar how to grip a club, but I was his first golf coach at Orangewood Christian School. As the school's athletic director, I remember having a parent's meeting early in the school year, and Peter Kuchar came up to me afterward and introduced himself. He asked whether our small school had a golf team, and I replied yes, I was a golf coach.

Peter said his son, a seventh grader, was excited about the game, and he hoped Matt could play on the high school team. We competed in a league in which seventh graders could play on varsity, so I said I'd love for Matt to try out for the team.

THE FIRST TEE SHOT

Matt came out, and during the preseason he was shooting in the mid-50s, maybe high 40s, for nine holes. This was a pretty good score for someone his age. We had a qualifier to see who would be the first six players on the team. Matt had a 48 that day and qualified as our sixth man. Of course, Peter was excited about Matt playing in his first match.

We teed off at DeBary Plantation, a nice course, and I remember Matt's first hole—a 400-yard par-4—like it was yesterday. On the number-one hole, he topped his first two shots into a ravine. He stuck down a third ball and barely got it up and over the ravine, and we watched it roll down the middle of the fairway. Then he took a wood and knocked the ball fairly close to the green, chipped up next to the pin, and one-putted for a snowman—an 8.

I thought I was making him nervous, so I went and watched my other players. I checked in on him on the fifth hole, and I learned that he had parred three out of the next four holes. Matt was five over at the time, but he ended up shooting 43 in his first nine holes of competitive golf.

We were in shock. We looked at each other and said we have got ourselves quite a player here. To come back from a bad beginning like that was really phenomenal. Meanwhile, Matt was smiling as he always does.

That was a great start to his playing career. The neat thing about Peter is that he never pushed Matt. He offered him an opportunity to play golf, and if Matt liked the sport, great. If not, he could do something else.

What set Matt apart from the other kids was his work ethic. He was always working on his short game. I told the kids on the team that they needed to spend 60 percent of their practice time around the green—chipping, pitching, and putting. "Do that, and you will take care of 60 percent of your score," I said.

Besides his short game, Matt had another reason for his success—his ability to put a bad shot behind him. He had this uncanny ability to forget terrible shots. I don't think he played his opponents as much as he played the course. Matt had a plan. He had an idea of what he wanted to do, and he did his best on every shot. I never saw him quit, and I saw my share of young kids quit after chili-dipping the ball into the water. Matt kept his chin up.

A lot of that has to do with his temperament. He's always been laid back, easygoing, and I think his parents certainly helped in cultivating that. I remember Peter coming to our matches and encouraging Matt whether he topped the ball or sank a long putt. I never saw him hard-nosed with Matt or ever confronting him. His mom, Meg, was also supportive. If Peter is Matt's biggest fan, then Meg is there right behind him.

The only thing I would say is we always knew Matt was a great athlete and had a lot of talent. But talent is a relative thing. We hope he's a role model, not only for kids today, but for everybody. We need more heroes. We need more role models. So if you choose Matt, you're making a pretty good choice. He's pretty special.

14

A Special Relationship

*L*et me tell you about another father-son duo who have accomplished as much, in my eyes, as Peter and Matt Kuchar.

Sports agents and golf companies won't be knocking down Mike Bearden's door to sign up his son, Tommy, to multiyear endorsement contracts. Augusta National and the U.S. Open won't be sending invitations for Tommy to play in their prestigious tournaments. But none of this matters to Mike, the father of a mentally handicapped son with hearing problems.

Tommy is the youngest of five children, and he has grown up playing golf with his three older brothers. The Beardens live in Caro, Michigan—the Great Lake State's "thumb area" about seventy-five miles north of Detroit. When spring arrives, Mike and Tommy, who is twenty years old, play at least once a week.

Tommy has something to play for. He participates in Special Olympics events, and a big moment came several years ago when he played in the World Special Olympics in New Haven, Connecticut, where special athletes from 138 countries came to compete. In his age-group division (fifteen to sixteen), Tommy was placed in a group with thirty to forty boys.

Tommy competed in a twenty-seven-hole tournament played at the Yale University golf course. Mike and his wife, Robin, followed Tommy around the course, but parents were not allowed to talk or advise the competitors. Only the caddies—volunteers from the Starter sporting goods company and the sponsor of the event—could converse with the players.

On one hole, Tommy struck two nice shots to leave himself with ninety yards of the flagstick. Tommy walked up to his ball and pulled out a 3-iron—and Mom and Dad began pulling out their hair. As Tommy commenced his preshot routine, the caddie noticed that his young Special Olympian was way overclubbed for such a short distance.

"Whoa," said the caddie. "Hit this."

The caddie handed Tommy his 7-iron. The teenager knocked it right on the green, and Mike and Robin squealed with delight.

Tommy shot 58 that day, and put together with his two previous rounds, captured third place and the bronze medal for his division. He also pocketed a huge helping of confidence. "After the Special Olympics, we saw Tommy's 'I can do it' level really rise," said Mike. "Golf has been such a great help to Tommy, but not only with his confidence. He has learned what it takes to play a game in which he has to practice and keep at it. He knows that when he makes a bad shot, he's got another one coming up, and that next shot will be better."

Starting Out

What advice does Mike have for parents of children with physical and mental handicaps? What encouragement can he bring to these families?

"Golf is one of the few sports that handicapped kids can play with their parents," said Mike. "The first thing I would say to parents is that you'll never know if they can swing a golf club and hit a ball if they don't try. The first thing we did with Tommy was get him a putter when he was six years old and let him make putts on the living room carpet. Once I saw him enjoying that, I took him to the practice green and taught him to putt the ball into the cup. It was then that he started formulating in his mind what this game is all about."

The key for Mike infecting Tommy with the golf bug was doing this sport together. Before Tommy could really play, Mike took him out on the course and let him ride as long as he wanted. Occasionally, he would let him putt or try a short pitch. At first, swinging a club and putting the clubface squarely on the ball proved to be a difficult task. Tommy became one frustrated grade-school youngster.

Obviously, Tommy was not blessed with tons of hand-eye coordination, and a golf swing can be a fairly complicated endeavor for even the most gifted athletes. Yet through Mike's patient approach, Tommy developed a solid swing by the time he entered adolescence.

"Tommy likes to study things," said Mike. "He gets up there and makes sure his stance is right and he's holding the club correctly. Then he looks to see whether he is aiming correctly. Sometimes he looks to me to make sure he's lined up correctly."

When Mike and Tommy go out and play nine holes together during the twilight hours (they enjoy looping small 9-hole public courses that cost seven to ten dollars a round), they are continuing a father-son tradition that began when Mike's dad took him out on the course. "Dad could have been a pro when he was young, back in the Walter Hagen days. But his father told him he had to go to college and get an education; besides, professional golf was just beginning in the 1930s and 1940s. Dad was a great natural athlete, a scratch golfer, and he taught me to play the game. I remember him saying that golf is a game in which all the shots are different, and that I had to learn all those different shots—coming out of sand traps and drawing the ball or making it fade. He really taught me to do those things."

Mike's dad also taught him some lessons that he has passed on to his sons:
1. Golf is a game you have to work at constantly. For that reason, it's not a boring sport.
2. You can count on every round of golf being different: sometimes good, sometimes not so good. Life is a lot like that.
3. Never get disgusted with golf, because tomorrow's another day.
4. The rewards will come. Just keep working at the correct way of playing.

Hitting Great Shots

Every year Mike and Tommy play together in the Michigan State Special Olympics golf tournament, competing in the "Unified" division, which allows the special athlete to choose a partner. Tommy always picks his father.

The first year they played together, the Beardens started their final round on the number one hole, a 143-yard par-3. The local Special Olympics committee introduced the father-son team to polite applause from the two or three dozen people standing around the first tee.

Mike worried about first-hole jitters.

"You'll do just fine, Tommy. Just take a whack at it."

Tommy reached for a 5-iron and let it fly. The ball landed on the green and rolled within two feet of the hole.

Tommy was so excited he could barely contain himself. "We're going to have a good day, Dad!"

The Beardens had a *great* day, and Tommy won a coveted gold medal in his division, the first of two that he has hung in his bedroom.

It's father-and-son moments like these that cause a lump to form in Mike's throat. "But you want to know the best part of playing golf with Tommy?" he asked. "It's the time we spend together. Golf is not something you spend a half hour doing with one of your kids. No, you get to spend two to five hours together and use that time to talk to each other. Between shots there's a great competitiveness, but it's also a great time of fellowship. Tommy saw the love I have for the game and caught the fever. Now he loves it too!"

Mike is a good player who plays to a 10-handicap, so to make the competition more fair, he hits a 7-iron off the tee so he will never outdrive Tommy. Then they walk up to their balls and have a relatively "equal" shot to the green. Doesn't Mike sound like a loving father? This is a dad who will downclub so he doesn't outhit his son. I say that's a demonstration of a father's love for his son.

The Special Olympics

Each state has a Special Olympics office, usually located at the state capitol or in major cities. Many public school systems have a Special Olympics program, and you can contact them for information.

Special Olympics programs are open to anyone with mental or physical handicaps, including wheelchair capabilities.

You can contact Special Olympics Headquarters by calling 202-628-3630 or e-mailing info@specialolympics.org.

Another highlight of the Beardens' golf season is playing in the local Special Olympics golf tournament held in Michigan's Tuscola County. The tournament benefits Special Olympics events throughout the year. A couple of years ago, Mike was playing with Tommy, and they came to the "prize hole"—a 157-yard par-3 in which a hole-in-one earned a new car or truck. Winner's choice.

"I'm going to win me a pick-up truck," said Tommy, lifting a 5-wood out of his bag.

Tommy waggled his wood, then made his swing. The ball flew on a trajectory right toward the pin . . . and settled seven feet from the hole. While I would love to be able to write that Tommy poked the ball into the hole, he had to settle for the second-closest shot of the day. The backslaps and high fives he received from his brothers were a nice consolation prize.

Don't worry, Tommy. You'll win a truck next time!

15

FAIRWAY TO DIVERSITY

I once met motivational speaker Zig Ziglar, who loves to play golf, when he spoke to the players before a PGA Tour stop. Zig has been called the most successful, charismatic, and influential speaker of our time, and I couldn't agree more with that assessment. Born in 1927, Zig grew up in Yazoo City, Mississippi, in a single-parent home. His mother milked the cows, cooked breakfast before daylight, put in a full day around the house, and quilted long after the kids had gone to bed.

Mama Ziglar also made sure the kids were in church, and she constantly reminded the children that God created everyone equal in his eyes—a philosophy not readily accepted in Mississippi, one of the most racist states in the country.

"In my childhood," said Zig, who is white, "I saw some kids calling a sixty-five-year-old black man 'boy.' That was the mind-set. That was the racial prejudice at the time. But my mother always told us, 'One of these days you will stand in front of a color-blind Lord. Until then, you will treat your black brothers and sisters with respect and with dignity.'"

I wish everyone could have been raised under those godly principles, but unfortunately, this has not been the case. Golf, with its blue-blood beginnings and walled-off country club history, has purposely discriminated against the poor, against minorities, and against women throughout much of the twentieth century. In fact, the PGA Tour was "whites only" until 1960, when Charlie Sifford broke the color barrier at age thirty-eight—past his prime, unfortunately. As great a game as golf is, the way the golf powers treated minorities in years past has left an indelible blotch mark on the sport.

I'm happy to report, however, that steps are being taken to welcome women and minorities to the game. This is good news, especially to the swelling ranks of the black middle class. Black golfers make up only 3 percent of the nation's golfers, but that's a 60 percent increase from the late 1980s, when only 1.8 percent of the nation's golfers were black. The Hispanic population comprises 2 percent of golfers.

Another step in the right direction was the formation of the National Minority Golf Foundation in the mid-1990s. It was initially headed by John Merchant, the first African-American to serve on the U.S. Golf Association's executive committee. Unfortunately, funding problems have plagued the National Minority Golf Foundation since its inception.

Let me put a human face on what golf outreach to minorities is all about. Renée Powell, one of the first black women to play the LPGA Tour, spends five weeks each summer teaching golf to mostly African-American and Hispanic kids from low-income neighborhoods in Cleveland. Approximately sixty kids a week participate in the Monday-through-Friday golf camps at Metro Park, a Cleveland municipal course. Kids earn the right to go to the camp by earning good grades and having high attendance marks. The camp is funded through a grant from PGA of America.

Renée says a typical camper is Maria, a high school student whose mother died of a stroke during camp. After her mother's untimely demise, Renée could reach out to her. The following year, when Maria confided that her father had been seeing someone else and wasn't making much time for her and her little brother, Renée made herself available to talk.

"Some of our kids come from dysfunctional families," said Renée. "We have kids who have their grandparents raising them or their aunts and uncles. We also have kids who are raising themselves in a very tough world. For instance, we had one young man in our program who had his jacket taken at school by gunpoint. For some reason, he ran after the kid who had stolen his jacket, and when he caught him, the other boy pointed a gun and shot him in the face.

"But you know what?" said Renée. "We use golf to teach these kids that they can do something on their own, which builds up their self-esteem and self-confidence. Hitting a golf ball gives them great self-satisfaction and helps them realize that they are somebody special."

When Renée is not overseeing the summer camp, she teaches lessons and runs the pro shop at Clearview Golf Club, a public course in East Canton, Ohio. Ask her why she's seeing more minorities taking up golf, and she replies with two words: "Tiger Woods."

For those of you who have been locked away in a mountain cabin without electricity for the last few years, Tiger Woods is a walking billboard for the new face of golf. His racial makeup is the quintessential American melting pot: his father, Earl Woods, is half-black, one-quarter Native American, and one-quarter Chinese; his mother, Kultida, is half-Thai, one-quarter Chinese and one-quarter white. Then there's the intangible: Tiger's a good-looking young man with a toothy grin.

With Tiger popping up everywhere in Nike TV advertisements, tens of thousands of kids have begun flocking to driving ranges with hand-me-down clubs in hand. Golf pros from Portland, Oregon, to Portland, Maine, have reported a tidal wave of juniors swelling their lesson programs.

Renée Powell noticed the influx of young players at her municipal facility. "Boys and girls identify with Tiger Woods because he's a young minority man who didn't grow up as a rich kid. Now he's playing what has been considered a white man's sport. 'Tigermania' has helped golf compete with sports like soccer and basketball."

> ### The Ultimate Link
>
> The USGA Foundation's Junior Golf Web site, www.JuniorLinks.com, maintains a master database of junior golf programs available throughout the United States. The PGA assisted in providing the content for this site with its "Golf It Up Brochure," one of the most popular documents on the site with more than ten thousand downloads.
>
> This site is filled with all kinds of incredible stuff for kids from games to rules to individual junior golfers' profiles and spotlights. Through this Web site, your child and you can have access to the total world of junior golf. So check it out and have a blast. Just go to JuniorLinks.com.

Golf, if given a chance, can compete very well with other sports, but kids need a place to play. Representatives from the PGA Tour, USGA, LPGA Tour, PGA of America, the Tiger Woods Foundation, and Augusta National Golf Club have rallied behind a program called the First Tee—a World Golf Village initiative dedicated to providing affordable golf access to those who otherwise might not have the opportunity to play.

Since its inception in 1997, the First Tee has opened 122 facilities and has introduced the game of golf to more than 170,000 young people since the year 2000. The program's focus is to give young people of all backgrounds an opportunity to develop, through golf and character education, life-enhancing values such as honesty, integrity, and sportsmanship.

The First Tee program has plans on the board to build public facilities at one hundred sites over the next few years, including one in my home state of Indiana, where plans are afoot to transform a 170-acre slag heap in Hammond into a sparkling eighteen-hole public course, driving range, practice range, and clubhouse.

Pastor J. Calaway (a great golfing name, isn't it?), of the Hammond First Assembly of God Church, is a 30-handicapper who enjoys playing golf and helping inner-city kids get into the game. "I don't want to sound snooty," he told interviewer Debbie Becker, with *Golf Digest,* "but golf is an etiquette sport. It teaches respect. You have to respect others, the ball, the lie, the turn. It keeps kids out of trouble while they learn at the same time. For so long, it's been a rich man's game. This program allows these kids to brush elbows with people they've never met before."

Harvey's Best Lesson

When 1995 Masters winner Ben Crenshaw was a junior player, he witnessed an incident between his teacher, Harvey Penick, and a Houston country club member.

Ben was hitting some balls under Harvey's watchful eye when the club member started yelling at a young Hispanic man picking up balls on the range.

"Get out of there!" he bellowed, gesturing with his hands. "Move!"

Harvey walked over to the man, put his head down, and said, "Sir, I'd appreciate if you would not talk that way to that young man. He is just as much a part of this golf course as you are."

Ashley Smith-Moore, a ninth-grader, is a Hammond teen who is beginning to see how golf can change people's lives, including her own. "Golf isn't a sport where your pants sag down to your knees, your hat is turned backwards, and you have a boombox in your hand," she said. "I can't wait until I can bring my father to this site and teach him how to play golf."

Someone once asked Charlie Sifford what he thought about the First Tee program. "I wish they had this when I was a kid," he said.

I'm sorry, Charlie, that golf wasn't there for you as a youngster. My hope is that we will be able to do something for the next generation of golfers—black, white, brown, and yellow.

There is no substitute for the quality instruction that you can get from a Professional Golfers Association (PGA) or Ladies Professional Golf Association (LPGA) Golf Junior Program. I'm also listing other organizations that have made outreach to minorities a priority.

Professional Golfers Association (PGA) is made up of forty-one sections scattered throughout the country. Each section has its own junior golf program director. These directors are in tune with the numerous Junior Golf activities throughout their areas. They would be happy to help direct your child and you to just the right kind of beginning program.

Web site: You can go to the Web site at www.PGA.com and get all the information that you need to find the PGA contact person in your area of the country who can direct you toward quality golf instruction and junior activities.

Address: PGA of America, 100 Avenue of Champions, Palm Beach Garden, FL 33418

Phone, National Headquarters: 561-624-8400

The Ladies Professional Golfers' Association (LPGA) has formed a partnership with the United States Golf Association called the LPGA-USGA Girls' Golf. This year-round, developmental junior golf program was formed to create a network for girls to learn how to play golf, make friends, and sample competition in a positive and supportive learning environment. As the only national initiative of its kind just for girls, the program provides the opportunities to develop skills, progress in golf, and have fun while establishing a lifelong interest in the game.

Web site: LPGA-USGA@FANS.LPGA.com

Address: LPGA, 100 International Golf Drive, Daytona Beach, FL 32124-1092

Phone number: 904-274-2600

The United States Golf Association (USGA) is a leader in providing materials and information for junior golfers. It is a must to have your kids become familiar with the fun rulebooks that the USGA provides along with many other great informational sources.

Web site: www.USGA.com

Address: USGA, Box 508, Farhills, NJ 07931-0708

Phone number: 1-800-223-0041

Hook-a-Kid on Golf is another fantastic golf youth organization that has programs all over the United States to get young people into the game. Not only do they have golf programs, but they also have a fantastic parks and recreation program called Start Smart Golf. This unique program is designed to help parents teach kids ages five to seven the game of golf. It uses a unique game called SNAG, which stands for Starting New at Golf. SNAG uses soft, fuzzylike tennis balls and big plastic-headed clubs and a whole system of Velcro-type flagsticks to shoot at. The youngsters really have fun learning and developing their skills. This program also allows for personal growth. As Kristin Pollard the program director for the Berlin-Kensington YMCA in Kensington, Kentucky, says, "We would have mom and dad swinging the clubs, and I would catch them hitting a few balls themselves afterward. I think they enjoyed it as much the kids did." Now that is what this book is all about. Hook-A-Kid on Golf is part of the National Alliance for Youth Sports.

Web site: www.NAYS.org/StartSmart

Address: Hook-A-Kid on Golf, 2050 Vista Parkway, West Palm Beach, FL 33411

Phone number: 1-800-729-2057

The First Tee is another fabulous national golf program for kids. It's a nonprofit organization that provides affordable access to golf and instills in young people life-enhancing values such as honesty, integrity, sportsmanship, and respect, all through the game of golf. The idea is to offer opportunities for improvement in the quality of life and create a platform where children can increase their potential for success. The First Tee was formed in November 1997 and is supported by all the world's leading golf organizations. The First Tee expects to have 250 dedicated First Tee golf facilities, plus five international and 500 affiliate golf course relationships with existing courses.

Web site: www.TheFirstTee.org

Address: First Tee, World Golf Village, 425 South Legacy Trail, St. Augustine, FL 32092

Phone number: 904-940-4300

Another wonderful opportunity educational opportunity for your kids and you would be to pay a visit to the **World Golf Hall of Fame** in St. Augustine, Florida. This will really give the kids a feeling for the history of the game. It's a fantastic place to go with exhibits that are designed to appeal to nongolfers as well as avid golfers, youngsters as well as seniors.

Just a few things you can do are:

- putt on an 1880s-style putting green with a wooden-shafted putter and gutta-percha ball.
- see highlights of golf's greatest moments in a mini-theater.

- stand up to the pressure of TV cameras, commentators, and crowd noise while you try to sink a final putt and win the World Golf Open. Plus they have an incredible par 3, eighteen-hole real grass putting course. It is an ultimate destination for kids and parents.

  Web site: www.WorldGolfHallofFame.com

  Address: World Golf Hall of Fame, 1 World Golf Place, St. Augustine, FL 32092

  Phone number: 904-940-4000

National Minority Golf Foundation

Web site: www.nmgf.org

Address: National Minority Golf Foundation, 7226 North 16th St., Suite 210, Phoenix, AZ 85020

Phone number: 602-943-8399

National Minority Junior Golf Scholarship Association

Web site: www.nmjgsa.org

Address: National Minority Junior Golf Scholarship Association, 120 W. Osborn Rd., Suite B, Phoenix, AZ 85013

Phone number: 602-258-7851

National Minority College Golf Scholarship Fund

Address: National Minority College Golf Scholarship Fund, 2000 E. 9th St., Suite 1235, Cleveland, OH 44115

Phone number: 216-646-4485

Tiger Woods Foundation

Web site: www.tigerwoods.com, click on Tiger Woods Foundation logo

Address: Tiger Woods Foundation, 7506 Slate Ridge Blvd., Reynoldsburg, OH 43068

Phone: 614-856-9460

There are many other organizations that deal with special needs children such as the Special Olympics, Disabled Kids, The Blind Golfers, Blind Junior Golfers, and many others. I have attempted to list some of the important ones, but the list could go for pages and pages. If you go online and do a search for "Junior Golf," you will find hundreds of programs dealing with junior golf around the country and the world. There really should be no excuse for a parent not having total access to the junior golf network.

16

WHEN OLD MAN WINTER TEES IT UP

I'm fortunate to live in the year-round, golf-rich environment of Orlando, home to seventy-five courses. Nonetheless, I recognize that many readers of this book reside in northern climes where they experience something called "the four seasons." How can you keep golf interest high when the clubs are tucked away in the attic four to six months a year?

I do have some answers, although you might think that's like a Florida fisherman advising Minnesotans on how to ice fish. Despite having lived in the Sunshine State for more than thirty years, I haven't forgotten what it was like to grow up in Indiana, where Old Man Winter took the clubs out of our hands from November until March.

I'll tell you one thing: golfing families remain excited about their sport year-round, even in snow country. This was made clear to me a few years ago when I flew to Minneapolis in the dead of winter to conduct a clinic at a consumer golf show held inside the Metrodome, home of the Minnesota Vikings and Minnesota Twins.

I found myself on a platform erected next to the bleachers with a couple of thousand parents and their kids watching me do my usual shtick with the hula hoops and the house mops and the hockey sticks. I thought the hockey stick swing analogy would resonate in Minnesota, home of ten thousand frozen lakes.

I took my big goalie stick and made several demonstration swings, each one faster than the last. Suddenly, to my horror, the *L* end of the stick flew off the handle and whirlybirded into the audience. The whipping blade struck a golfing parent named Michael Bark in the forehead, slicing him like a scythe. He crumpled to the floor, and blood poured from his wound. Fortunately, a hockey team trainer was sitting beside him, and he stemmed the blood flow with a handkerchief until EMTs arrived on the scene.

It was a chore for paramedics to reach him in the stands, but they eventually placed Michael on a gurney and rushed him to a local hospital, where it took doctors seventeen stitches to close the wound!

I felt horrible, and when my clinic was finished, I called Michael at the hospital to see how he was doing. We had a friendly chat, and Michael told me that he and his family had driven more than two hundred miles from Washburn, Wisconsin, to attend my golf clinic and check out the latest golf paraphernalia. I also learned that his elementary school-aged children, Matthew and Amy, were top-ranked junior golfers in northwestern Wisconsin and play on the Minnesota Junior PGA Tour.

I've kept in touch with Michael since that horrible accident, and I asked him to share some ideas on how a golfing family can keep their interest level higher than the snowdrifts outside their front door.

Here is what Michael told me:

We live in Washburn, Wisconsin, a town of twenty-five hundred people. Our nearest golf facility is the Ashland Elks Golf Course, ten miles away in Ashland. It's a links-style public course that recently expanded from nine to eighteen holes, and rates are reasonable—seventeen dollars for eighteen holes, with generous discounts for junior members.

I've played golf since I was a young boy, having been introduced to the game by my father. Dad has passed away, but I still get emotional when I think about our special times on the golf course.

After thirteen years of marriage, my wife, Colleen, and I adopted a beautiful, three-week-old son whom we named Matthew. Then we learned that Colleen was pregnant! When Amy was born eight months later, we felt like we had been blessed with twins.

I couldn't wait to get a golf club into their hands. Matt was sturdy enough at age two to putt in the living room and swing a club outdoors. Amy always had a variety of interests, and her desire for golf blossomed later than her brother's.

Matt and Amy started getting involved in junior golf programs by the time they started reading. Colleen and I strongly believe in letting our kids seek out other interests as well, like cross-country and downhill skiing, soccer, and school and church activities such as music and choir. This is helping them be well-rounded individuals.

There's no danger of becoming a year-round golf nut in our neck of the woods. The Ashland course usually closes by Halloween, which is all trick or no treat for us since Matt and Amy play three, four, five times a week when they're not in school.

Then we watch the snow pile up. We receive 90 to 130 inches of snow each winter, with periods of below-zero temperatures and highs rarely topping thirty degrees. We can't afford to take a winter golf trip to Florida or Arizona, so we do other things to keep up our golf interest. We receive three or four golf magazines each month at home. We watch golf instructional videos, which is how I heard about Wally. Whenever Matt and Amy come home with an assignment to do a school report, they always choose a golf-related subject. That means heading over to the local library and checking out a few golf books or perusing our comprehensive golfing library at home.

Colleen often puts pictures of the kids playing at golf tournaments on our family picture wall or refrigerator, and both kids enjoy hanging posters in their bedrooms of guys like Tiger Woods and Tom Lehman. One winter, Colleen made a quilt using squares from numerous T-shirts the kids received at junior tournaments.

Unfortunately, our ceilings are not high enough to practice a full golf swing, although Matt tries to practice his chipping every now and then. The kids do like to putt on the living room carpet and downstairs in the basement, where we have a three-hole "course" set up. If we really have the itch to hit balls, we can drive eighty miles to Duluth, Minnesota, and knock irons inside the Golf Skydome. I guess it's better than nothing.

When visiting Duluth, we generally spend the day shopping, making sure we drop by Marty Irving's Golf Shop and department stores that carry golf equipment. Our day in Duluth wouldn't be complete without a quick stop at Play It Again Sports, where we hunt for deals on used equipment.

As winter winds blow off Lake Superior and the temperatures drop below zero, that's a good time to put another log on the fire and reach for a good golf book. We may watch home movies taken at various tournaments, play golf on the home computer, or go to bed early and dream heavenly thoughts of lush green fairways and making a long putt for birdie.

The highlight of our winter is playing in two "ice" golf tournaments. The first is the Doc Langford Golf on Ice tournament held on Chequamegom Bay of Lake Superior. A local group goes out on the ice and plows the "fairways," then uses an ice auger to make the "hole"—six inches wide by six inches deep, with a long pole marking the hole. It's a nine-hole, par-36 layout, but you can only use one club. Matt, Amy, and I (Colleen's too smart to play) take our 5-irons and orange balls and have a great time.

We have to dress warm since the tournament is rarely played in temperatures above freezing. We don our snowmobile suits, Sorrel boots, stocking caps, leather chopper mittens, and flail away.

The other winter event is sponsored by the Iron River Snowmobile Club, who put on a benefit tournament on a frozen inland lake thirty miles from town. The "course" is much more natural because the fairways are not plowed. Competitors use tennis balls, and of course, "winter rules" are in play!

Then it's the long wait until our Ashland course opens, traditionally around April 15. Many of us golfers can't wait that long to tee it up, however, so every year more than one hundred of us drive three hours to the "banana belt" regions of Wisconsin where they are already playing golf.

The towns of Eau Claire and Hayward usually have a two-week jump on us, and right around the first of April, we travel to Hayward for the Sarver Open, a little tournament essentially for people from Washburn. It's strictly social golf, and you see a lot of rusty swings out there, but we sure have fun. The temperatures are often cool, and many times we have to wear stocking caps and gloves, but we know the days of warm sunshine, the smell of freshly mowed grass, and quiet afternoons strolling the deep-green fairways will soon be ours.

Wasn't Michael's story great? No wonder Minnesota and Wisconsin have the highest number of golfers per capita than anywhere else in the United States. His story reminded me of growing up in Indianapolis. In those days, there was no winter golf, so I wrestled, which got me in great shape for golf season.

Anyway, if you live in a four-seasons climate, here are some ideas:

• *Play other sports that develop hand-eye coordination.* When I was a youngster, Indianapolis didn't have indoor training centers where you could hit balls into tall nets. Besides wrestling, I played Ping-Pong for hours and hours in our family basement, which did wonders for my hand-eye coordination. Pool is another good sport for developing coordination. Bob Murphy, who had a great PGA career in the 1960s and 1970s, played pool every night as a youngster, and he was the best putter I ever saw.

• *Take your winter vacation in the Sun Belt.* If you can afford it, fly or drive the family during Thanksgiving, Christmas, or the February Presidents' holidays to a place where you can play golf. Several companies specialize in golf packages

(GolfPac at 888-848-8941 or www.golfpacinc.com is one), and all sorts of deals can be found in the classified sections of golf magazines or on the Internet.

That's doesn't mean you have to stay at some fancy resort, blowing a huge chunk of the family's annual vacation budget. Do you have family or good friends you could stay with? Who knows, you could always reciprocate and have the cousins come to your place for some snowmobiling and sledding, sports generally unknown to those below the Mason-Dixon line.

• *Check out your indoor hitting areas.* Lots of golf shops have indoor hitting zones in the basement. Sure, it can get pretty boring striking the ball into a hanging green tarp with a white bull's-eye painted in the center, but it will keep you and your children's swing grooved. Hit ten balls and then switch partners to keep the boredom factor down.

Some northern towns have domes. Mike Bearden, the Michigan father whom you met in chapter 13, loves taking his handicapped son, Todd, to an indoor hitting dome to strike their irons. At least inside a dome you get to see most of the flight of the ball before it hits the net.

• *Play virtual golf.* The advent of golf simulators—indoor hitting rooms where you strike a real ball toward a ten-foot-high, fourteen-foot-wide projection screen— have made indoor golf incredibly realistic. Sensors underneath the hitting mat measure the angle of your club, club speed, and other variables. That information is sent to a computer, and in nanoseconds you see the flight of your virtual ball streaking toward the picturesque number 16 at Cypress Point, the famous par-3 on the Pacific Ocean. If the computer determines that you swung well, then you're on the green.

Golf simulators have made great strides in recent years. You can hear balls bounce off tree branches and shots splash into water. You can play Pebble Beach, Spyglass Hill, St. Andrews, Banff, or dozens of other memorable courses. The putting on these golf simulators still leaves something to be desired, but I think they're a great way to spend a snowy afternoon with your son or daughter.

The cost is generally twenty dollars an hour—per group, not per person. You can pay up to forty dollars an hour in expensive northeast cities such as New York

City. There are more than 415 indoor golf centers operating 900 golf simulators across the U.S. and Canada. Many of these golf simulators are booked eighteen hours a day from 7:00 A.M. to 1:00 A.M., so call ahead for your "tee time."

• *Have a computerized analysis taken of your golf swings.* Besides playing in golf simulators, you and your children can have your swings checked from top to bottom by swing analyzers that measure the clubhead at the time of ball impact, the vertical and horizontal look of your backswing and forward swing, and ball speed. A good golf pro should be able to incorporate all this information into ways that can help you improve your swing. A computerized analysis is a great way to groove your swings during the off-season.

• *Play when it's marginal.* I stretched the golf season as long as I could growing up in Indiana. If my course was still open at Thanksgiving, I was out there. As long as you dress for the cold and don't have much wind, you can play when the air temperature dips into the thirties. You won't be alone. According to a National Golf Foundation survey of six hundred golfers, one-third said they would play if the temperature was thirty-five degrees or lower.

• *Go indoors.* Do you have any rooms with twelve-foot ceilings? If so, you and the kids can swing a practice club and hit whiffle balls. Some golf shops and mail-order catalogs carry those "Instant Info" trainers that "hold" a ball in place so you have something to hit. You can also purchase something called the "Ultimate Putting System," which has a nine-foot carpet green, a regulation hole, and an automatic return. You can always have putting contests on the living room rug. Just watch for that break next to the fireplace.

• *Go outdoors.* If you have a sunny day with highs sneaking into the forties, you can always bring out a pop-up net and hit balls into it.

• *Go to the Net.* Nothing to do on a stormy Sunday afternoon? Noodle around the Internet at some of your favorite golf sites. May I suggest taking a peek at www.wallyarmstrong.com?

• *Keep watching golf on TV.* I know it can be painful when it's blizzarding outside and you tune in the sun-baked Bob Hope Chrysler Classic in Palm Springs during the PGA Tour stop every January. Yet watching tournament golf on TV can keep the kids' excitement level high as they follow their favorite players. Don't forget that kids learn by imitating, and their eyes are soaking in the movements of the pros' swings.

• *Play winter golf.* Some inveterate golfers go the extra mile and play winter golf tournaments like the ones Michael Bark described. If nothing is that organized in your area, you and your children can always trudge out to a snow-covered course (or nearby field) and hit orange balls toward a "hole." Winter golf is not a game many people want to play, but once or twice a winter it could be fun.

• *Rent golf videos.* Too stormy to venture outside? Have a Saturday night with nothing to do? Depending on your cinematic taste in humor, you could rent one of several silly golf movies available.

If you're really hard up for something golf-related to watch, you can always tune in one of those golf infomercials that pop up on cable TV every now and then. Careful, though. You might end up buying some Adams Tight Lies fairway woods or Medicus Double-Hinged Clubs.

• *Subscribe to the Golf Channel.* More and more cable systems around the country are offering the Golf Channel, a twenty-four-hour premium golf channel featuring tournaments, replays of classic rounds from tournaments past, instructional pieces, interviews, and a news roundup show. Cost is usually around ten dollars a month, except for those fortunate people who live in areas where the Golf Channel is part of their basic package!

17

WATCHING
THE PROS PLAY

No matter how much golf you watch on TV, or even if your set is permanently tuned to the Golf Channel, there is nothing like going out and watching the pros play in person. You can't get an appreciation for how far they hit or how routinely they extricate themselves from trouble when you're watching from the La-Z-Boy.

I'm not talking about only the PGA Tour with its young lions and veteran stars; I'm also talking about the Ladies Professional Golf Association (LPGA) Tour, the Champions Tour, and even the minor-leagues like the Nationwide Tour. Few other professional sports allow fans to get as close to the players—so close that you can overhear the pro conversing with his caddie or course official. You can follow your favorite pro or stake out a place and wait for the players and their caddies to come to you.

You and your youngsters can learn a few things watching the pros up close and personal. It's interesting to watch them work in their "office," where the pros are in no hurry to finish their workday. The pros are exceedingly patient. Watching how the pros meticulously align themselves to the ball can remind us to think more before automatically drawing back our club and hitting away.

The pros have a game plan, and if you sit on a particular hole, watch where the drives land and how they play their approach shots to the green. Which quadrant on the green do they seem to be aiming for?

If you want to be a spectator, you need a game plan. Follow this one:

• *Try to attend on one of the pro-am days.* Pro-ams happen Tuesdays and Wednesdays (sometimes just the latter day). Pro-am tournaments are basically practice rounds for the pros, who are paired with amateurs who've ponied up three thousand dollars for the privilege of knocking it around with a Mark O'Meara or a Colin Montgomerie. The money goes toward a small purse but is mainly earmarked for local charities.

I was called the King of the Pro-Ams in my playing days because the meager winnings augmented my prize money earnings. I also genuinely enjoyed meeting new people, and invariably I'd help some poor fellow, shaking like a leaf, get through the round. Playing with me was like getting a playing lesson.

Today's pros are playing for too much prize money from Thursday to Sunday to worry about a measly pro-am tournament, so they are generally loose and quick to banter with the gallery. The pros will sign autographs during the pro-am, but they will *never* sign during the regular tournament. During pro-ams, stake out a place between the green and the next tee box for autographs.

These Guys Are Good

Here's why professional golf is so popular:

- When golfers make a mistake, nobody is there to cover for them or back them up.
- There are no guaranteed contracts in the professional game; you are compensated in direct proportion to how well you play.
- Golf doesn't have free agents or players being traded.
- Golf doesn't change its rules to attract fans.
- Tiger Woods can hit a golf ball three times as far as Barry Bonds can hit a baseball.
- Professional golfers don't demand that taxpayers pay for the courses on which they play.
- You can watch the best players up close, all day, every day for no more than twenty-five or thirty dollars. A World Series ticket in the bleachers would cost close to two hundred dollars.
- Golfers don't beat each other up during the game, nor do you see bench-clearing brawls.
- Finally, the PGA Tour raises more money for charity in a year than the National Football League does in two.

Here are some other things you should know about autographs once the regular tournament starts:

1. Pros generally will not sign while warming up or while they are competing. Many sign *after* their round is over. A good place to catch pros after their round is when they mosey over to the driving range to hit extra balls.

2. Know that some pros willingly sign; others don't. How would you feel if you had a piece of paper and a Magic Marker thrust in your face every moment you were in the public eye? Autograph hounds can be wearisome. I do know this: saying "please" and "thank-you" will get noticed by the pro since many children have not learned good manners in this area.

3. Be different. Don't ask for autographs. Ask to shake their hands. You'll find many pros willing to look you in the eye and make small talk, which, to me, would be far more memorable.

• *Consider volunteering to be a marshal during the tournament.* If your children are sturdy teens and out of school, you all could become volunteer marshals. Your son or daughter could carry the big "player's sign" while they walk alongside Justin Leonard and Sergio Garcia. Best seats in the house.

• *Go early and watch the pros practice.* You are far from the maddening crowd when you arrive early—before 8:00 A.M. It's easy to run into the stars and fun to watch them warm up on the practice tee.

• *When you arrive, study a map of the course.* What is the most difficult hole? What is the course's signature hole? Personally, I like to watch the par-5 and par-3 holes for the following reasons:

1. On par-5s, the pros usually aim for the green on the second shot, so you often witness a variety of shots.

2. On par-3s, the pros usually have to deal with bunkers and water protecting the green, but they fire for the flag anyway, which can be especially exciting to watch.

I remember one time when Scott was around twelve years old, and we drove over to Jacksonville, Florida, to spend the day at the Tournament Player's

Championship at the TPC at Sawgrass. Number 17 is the signature hole; it's a medium-length par-3 with an island green. Miss the green and the ball goes *ker-plunk* into the water.

"Come on, Scott, I want to show you this hole," I said as we found a spot behind the tee box.

"How long is it, Dad?"

"It's playing 135 yards, but it's much more difficult than it looks."

"One hundred and thirty-five yards? I could make that."

"Scott, this is the hardest hole on the course."

"No, it isn't. It's only 135 yards."

Scott was a precocious player with an excellent short game for his age, but I wanted him to understand that lofting a wedge into the wind and hoping that it stays dry on a postage-stamp-sized island was more difficult than it appeared to be from behind the tee box. The previous day, I had read in the newspaper that thirty-five pros had rinsed their balls in the water, forcing them to trudge over to the drop area sixty yards from the green.

We waited for the first pro to hit. After a customary waggle or two, he fired a pitching wedge at the flag. The ball bounded on the green and rolled into the cup for a hole-in-one.

"Did you see that, Dad? I told you this hole was easy."

What could I say? That's tournament golf, and you never know what you'll see. A couple of years later, I took Blake with me to number 17, where we watched Len Mattiace, a shot or two off the lead, knock three balls into the drink and card a disastrous 9. The horror hole cost him $75,000 in prize money.

Len might have wanted to jump into the lake with his clubs, but he kept his chin up, which impressed everyone in the gallery when he pulled himself together and birdied 18. We can learn much from the pros' deportment and how they carry themselves around the course. Most professional golfers treat victory and defeat like an impostor, as Rudyard Kipling said in his famous poem.

• *Pick up a pairings list.* The tournament pairs up players in twosomes and threesomes. Is there a favorite pro you want to follow?

Inside the Ropes

If you attend a pro tournament and are looking for several good role models to follow, here are a few you can root for:

- *Davis Love III:* Playing at the very top of the game, Davis is often in contention on the back nine on Sunday afternoons.
- *Justin Leonard:* He may not be as long as the big hitters, but Justin plays an entertaining game and knocks down long putts.
- *Kenny Perry:* This good-ol' boy with a sweet swing has a sweet love for Jesus.
- *Tom Lehman:* Tom is a great Christian brother, and we roomed together during his first season on tour back in the mid-1980s. Tom won the British Open in 1996 and came within a shot or two of winning the U.S. Open on several occasions.
- *Paul Azinger:* A twelve-time winner on the tour, including one major, the PGA Championship, Paul is a cancer survivor who has stared death in the face.
- *David Gossett:* David is one of the young lions on tour who could be contending for a major soon.
- *Matt Kuchar:* I've already talked about Matt a couple of chapters ago, but he's a long hitter who's fun to watch around the green.
- *Bernard Langer:* I'll never forget the time Bernard won the Masters on Easter Sunday, and he said on national television how pleased he was to have won the day that we commemorate the resurrection of Jesus Christ.
- *Loren Roberts:* His colleagues say that he's one of the best putters on tour. When Loren gets hot with the flat stick, watch out!

The ladies tour has some wonderful Christian players as well. *Hilary Lunke,* the unknown who captured the U.S. Open in 2003, is a believer, as was one of the runners-up, *Angela Stanford.* Hall of Fame player *Betsy King,* who has six majors to her credit, has been vocal about her faith in Christ for years.

• *Purchase those little portable seats.* Having portable seats carries several advantages, the biggest one being that you get to rest your tired bones. At most tournaments, etiquette allows you to set the chair right behind the rope and return to it later.

• *Decide whether you're going to follow or camp out on a green.* Each way has its advantages. If you have a favorite golfer you love to watch, by all means follow him (or her). If you're going to follow Tiger Woods, however, be prepared not to see much of him since he attracts the largest gallery.

Camping out on a green and watching several playing groups come in can be fun. This is where you can get closest to the players—so close that you can sometimes eavesdrop on the discussions between player and caddie regarding how the putt will break. You can watch several different shots when you're around the green: the approach shot coming in, the bunker play, chipping around the fringe, and putts from almost every distance.

Check Out This Library

I love how the Bark family reads golf books during the dead of winter to keep the burning embers of golf devotion stoked.

Did you know there are a number of books out there that talk about golf and spiritual values? They would be perfect for your kids to read (and you, too, Mom and Dad). I'm talking about the golf devotional books that I've written (*In His Grip*, etc.) or inspirational stories about Christian golfers, of which there are quite a few on the PGA Tour.

If I can make one more shameless plug, it would be for another book of mine called *Heart of a Golfer*, which weaves life, golf, and God into one awesome lesson plan. *Heart of a Golfer* contains more than thirty-six lessons from the practice tee of golf to the eighteenth hole of life.

Finally, I have to tell you about the *Links Letter*, an excellent newsletter for which I'm proud to write an occasional column. This bimonthly magazine (which is also available electronically) features testimonies about pro tour players, plus insights from columnists such as Bobby Clampett, LPGA's Tracy Hanson, and PGA Tour chaplain Larry Moody.

The mission of *Links* is presented in an acronym drawing from each of the letters of the word:

- *L—love* for God and others. "Jesus replied: "'Love the Lord your God with all your heart and with all your soul and with all your mind.' This is the first and greatest commandment. The second is like it: 'Love your neighbor as yourself'"" (Matt. 22:37–39 NIV).
- *I—integrate* Christ's reign and integrity into all of life. "But seek first his kingdom and his righteousness, and all these things will be given to you as well" (Matt. 6:33).
- *N—network* friends together in Christ. "They devoted themselves to the apostles' teaching and to the fellowship, to the breaking of bread and to prayer" (Acts 2:42).
- *K—kindle* compassion for the poor and needy. "The King will reply, 'I tell you the truth, whatever you did for the least of these brothers of mine, you did for me'" (Matt. 25:40).
- *S—share* Christ through the great game of golf. "We are therefore Christ's ambassadors, as though God were making his appeal through us" (2 Cor. 5:20a).

You can check out www.linksplayers.com for more details, or call toll-free (800) 90-LINKS.

18

FINISHING STRONG

Chances are you never heard of Robert Lockhart, a New York linen merchant who emigrated from Scotland to the United States sometime before the 1880s. Lockhart often traveled by ship between New York and the British Isles to conduct business. During a late-summer 1887 trip to Scotland, Lockhart visited golf's Holy Grail—the Royal and Ancient Burgh of St. Andrews, where Scots had been playing golf for centuries.

Lockhart, a well-to-do businessman who had been exposed to golf in his younger days, walked into the golf shop on St. Andrews' grounds, where he found Old Tom Morris, the British champion, holding court. Old Tom made clubs by hand, and Lockhart picked out three woods, three irons, and two dozen gutta-percha balls.

Lockhart returned to his adopted hometown of Yonkers, New York, and when a midwinter thaw swept through the Northeast in late February 1888, he invited his two sons, Sydney and Leslie, to be the first persons to play golf in the New World. The date was Sunday, February 22, 1888. The following is Sydney's account, which originally appeared in *Fifty Years of American Golf* by H. B. Martin:

> One bright Sunday, Father, my brother Leslie, and myself went up to a place on the river which is now Riverside Drive. It was not a wilderness by any means, as I recall there was a mounted policeman near the spot Father selected as a teeing ground.

Father teed up the first little white ball, and selecting one of the long wooden clubs, dispatched it far down the meadow. He tried all the clubs, and then we boys were permitted to drive some balls too. One of Father's shots came dangerously close to taking the ear off an iceman, but the policeman did not arrest my father, and merely smiled. Later the cop asked if he could hit one of those balls, and naturally my father was more than pleased that he was so friendly. The officer got down off his horse and went through the motions of teeing up, aping Father in waggling and squaring off to the ball and other preliminaries. Then he let go and hit a beauty straight down the field, which went fully as far as any that Father had hit. Being greatly encouraged and proud of his natural ability at a game that involved a ball and stick, he tried again. This time he missed the ball completely, and then in rapid succession he missed the little globe three more times; so with a look of disgust on his face, he mounted his horse and rode away.

You know what I love about this story? The first recorded instance of golf being played in the United States involved a father-son outing!

I wonder if golf began that way back in the Middle Ages, when feudal lords— and their sons?—began chasing feather-filled balls through their pasturelands. Let's look back to golf's early days to see where we've come from and where we are going.

Many golf historians credit Scotland as being the cradle of golf when the game started to gain a following during the Industrial Age in the nineteenth century. The invention of a hard-shell ball (called the gutta-percha) in the 1850s made golf more affordable, although it remained the province of nobles and aristocracy. As the game grew in favor in the British Isles, several enterprising Scottish merchants immigrated to the United States and brought their love of golf with them, including Robert Lockhart, who, after that Washington's Day outing with his sons, rounded up several other Scots, including John G. Reid, to organize the first permanent golf club in 1888 in Yonkers. They named it St. Andrews Golf Club (no apostrophe) after St. Andrew's (with apostrophe) back in their homeland.

The sporting public was unimpressed; they viewed golf as a hobby for home-sick Brits. In 1894, however, A. G. Spalding & Bros., a company known for manufacturing mitts and bats for a new pastime called baseball, contracted British Open champion Harry Vardon to barnstorm the United States and drum up inter-est in golf—and sell a few sets of Spalding "golf sticks" along the way. The ploy worked marvelously. Everywhere Vardon went, magnificent crowds followed him, and newspapers offered breathtaking coverage. America was getting to know golf, and the increased demand for facilities spurred a golf construction boom.

Americans love underdog stories, and the improbable victory of twenty-year-old Francis Ouimet at the 1913 U.S. Open against the lions of British golf—Harry Vardon and Ted Ray—captured the imagination of the public. Ouimet, the son of middle-class parents, might have been born on the other sides of the tracks, but he beat the world's best at their own game.

The Roaring Twenties were good to golf, as course construction raised the number of golf courses to 5,700, with 400 in the state of New York alone. Then Robert T. Jones—Bobby Jones—came along and changed the face of golf forever. He was golf's first superstar and a magnetic personality who became known to Americans via newsreels shown in movie theaters.

The Great Depression, however, shuttered many country clubs and sent the sport into a sidespin that lasted all the way through World War II, when a global shortage of rubber halted all new ball construction. When World War II was over, however, the expanding middle class discovered golf all over again through a new medium—television. It certainly helped that the president of the United States, Dwight Eisenhower, was an avid golfer, and stars such as Ben Hogan and Arnold Palmer attracted widespread interest.

Arnie became the first of a string of telegenic golfers who are on a first-name basis with many Americans, and we know them as Arnie and Jack and Tom and Johnny and Greg and Tiger and Sergio (their last names are Palmer, Nicklaus,

Watson, Miller, Norman, Woods, and Garcia for those of you still getting up to speed). And where would women's golf be today without Babe Zaharias, Mickey Wright, Nancy Lopez, Annika Sorenstam, and Se Ri Pak? They are wonderful role models worthy of your children's emulation.

Which brings us to today. A game as good as golf isn't going to disappear from the face of the earth because golf *matters*. With the help of my good friend John Unger, here are some reasons why:

Golf matters because we are—first and foremost—moral and spiritual beings, and golf is among the most moral and spiritual of all games.

Golf matters because the games we play and the way we play them say a lot about who we are and what we value as individuals and as a society.

Golf matters because golf humbles us no matter who we are, titan or toddler, champion or duffer, allowing us to learn about humility and perspective, patience, and grace.

Golf matters because to play the game is to become part of something larger than ourselves, part of the culture of golf, which helps us understand the value of such things as rules, traditions, and a shared sense of history.

Golf matters because of its universal appeal to young and old, male and female, rich and poor, black and white. Golf reminds us that we are more alike than we are different.

Golf matters because it requires that we experience failure and learn many valuable lessons, foremost among them that it's OK to fail, so long as you get back up, dust yourself off, and try again.

Golf matters because it provides an increasingly rare opportunity in this day and age to experience in one place the three essential elements of moral education: (1) an awareness of the virtues that define a person of character; (2) examples of those traits as told through stories and real-life role models; and (3) an opportunity to practice and reinforce the habits of good character over a lifetime.

What makes golf a game above all others is the unhurried pace that allows relationships to deepen, friendships to form, memories to be made. What better game for a father-son, mother-son, father-daughter, mother-daughter, grandparent-grandchild?

Wayne Gretzky, perhaps hockey's greatest player of all time, lives with his family in a home overlooking the thirteenth fairway of Sherwood Country Club near Thousand Oaks outside Los Angeles. Wayne has caught the golf bug, as has his wife, Janet. They play nearly every day, and their three children take lessons at the club.

Listen to what Wayne wrote in a "My Shot" column in *Sports Illustrated*: "I have no aspirations to become the greatest golfer or athlete-golfer or hockey-golfer or even the best Gretzky golfer. I don't have that kind of passion for the game. Janet and I are perfectly happy playing a fivesome with the kids or an afternoon scramble with our neighbors Claude and Deborah Lemieux. Family and friends—that's what golf is all about to me."

That's great to hear, Wayne. You've got it right. To close this book, I would like to finish with a story by Bob Welch, an Oregon father of two boys. Bob's story captures the essence of what *The First Tee Shot* is all about for families.

Seizing the Moment

by Bob Welch

On a cool summer morning, two golfers blow on their cupped hands to ward off the chill. They stand on the tee and look ahead toward their target, lost somewhere in the yellowish light of sunrise. It's 6:00 A.M.

The hole is arrow-straight with a slight dogleg left at the end. Water left. Trees and beach grass right.

And lots of sand.

Lots and lots and lots of sand.

You see, this golf hole stretches seven miles long. It was created by my sixteen-year-old son and me by sticking a soup can in the sand about 12,320 yards north of my grandfather's beach cabin on the Oregon coast.

Par 72, we figure.

This sea monster makes the 948-yard sixth at Australia's Kooland Island Golf Course—the longest in the world, according to Guinness—look like a miniature golf hole by comparison.

But this challenge is more than man vs. monster. It's also father vs. son, as it's been since our toddler football games began nearly sixteen years ago.

Ryan steps to the first—and only—tee. Like a young gymnast, he fears nothing. *Thwack.* He hits one straight down the middle. *When did he get so strong?*

I step to the tee like a forty-one-year-old man who fears nearly everything, particularly the water trap on my left—the Pacific Ocean—that spans 64 million square miles and covers one-third of the earth's surface. When God made the sea and saw that it was good, He obviously wasn't taking my hook into consideration.

But I, too, hit straight and long. I may be aging, but I refuse to go gently into the good night.

The Thrill of Competition

We're off in the morning mist. The gallery is decidedly uninterested, as most of the feathery fans are too busy ripping the innards from washed-ashore crabs to pay much attention to us.

That's fine; we're not here for glory. We're here for the same reason one man in an office will shoot a crumpled memo into a wastebasket as if he were David Robinson. We're competition freaks who do crazy things involving sports. But we're also here because the father is increasingly aware that time and tide wait for no man.

He sees a son, who, Lord and admissions directors willing, will be off to college in a couple of years to do more mature things, like painting his entire upper body in school colors for home football games.

This father-son stuff won't go on forever, this dad has realized lately. He's heard all those sermons about parents being the bows and children being the arrows, and he knows the archer must soon let go. Plus, he's read the late golf guru Harvey Penick's book that encourages golfers to "Take dead aim." The axiom, the father has come to understand, goes beyond the golf course to life itself.

What's more, the same father determined months ago that a very low tide on this particular morning of the family vacation would stretch the fairway to its optimum width. A couple hundred yards is a gloriously wide margin of error for someone who once broke a car window with a snap hook.

Fairway Jaunt

Down the windless beach we head—two waves at different points in our journey to shore. I see Ryan as a silhouette against the eastern sky and think, *When did he get to be so tall?*

We each carry but one club—a driver, for maximum distance. I hit the ball farther in the air, but Ryan takes better advantage of the hard sand with line drives that hit and roll forever. At Big Creek, three miles after teeing off, he has a full stroke on me, 26 to 27.

We each wear a fanny pack filled with extra golf balls that unmask my spoken bravado. Ryan has packed three extra balls. Me? Twelve.

As the early morning sky turns light blue, the match remains tight. The sun bursts through the trees at the four-mile mark, turning the surf to a frothy white. The smoke from a state campground flavors the cool air.

We play Rules of Golf with Beach Alterations: Every shot may be placed on a wooden tee, of which we've brought many. But anything in the water—be it ocean, tide pool, creek, or lagoon—cannot be removed without a one-stroke penalty. Seaweed, logs, and dead gulls are not considered loose impediments and, thus, cannot be moved.

Hit, walk, hit, walk. The journey continues. Past motels. Past cabins. Past deep-thinking walkers who stroll the fairway as if they were on a beach.

We make small talk. In the months to come, as Ryan grows more independent, there will be time for deeper things; for now, it is enough that we comment on blocks of sandpipers, rib each other relentlessly about who will win, and compare hunger pains, which our Big Hunk candy bars soon fix.

Then it happens. Near Yaquina John Point, with a mile to go, disaster strikes Ryan. It is the long-distance golfer's equivalent of a sailor's mast breaking—his last tee snaps in half. He must now hit off the hard-pan sand with a driver, a difficult task.

Half of me wants to console him and loan him a tee; half of me wants to exploit this advantage for all its worth. Being the sensitive midlife father I am, I smile like the Grinch who stole Christmas and push the thrusters to Full Exploit. This is, after all, a kid who loves to beat me at everything from arm wrestling to Yahtzee; who only occasionally loans me *my* pickup; and who chides me for thinking POD is a medical acronym, not a Christian band.

I must cling to my dignity anyway I can get it.

Ryan doesn't grouse; he simply buckles down and does his best. *When did he get so mature?*

Clubhouse Finish

A hundred yards out, with the seaweed flag now in sight, we are dead even. Father and son. Sixty-two shots apiece. After each hitting four more shots, Ryan is twelve feet and I am three feet from the hole. The pressure mounts.

Ryan lines up his putt, steps over the ball, strokes and—misses. He looks to the sky in agony before tapping in for a 4-under-par 68.

So it comes to this: After seven miles and sixteen years, I can remain the Family Beach Golf King by making this simple putt.

I stand over the ball that I teed off with four hours earlier. (Amazingly, Ryan and I have each used only one, though the sand has all but worn off the dimples.)

All is quiet. A few crabbers watch curiously from their boats on nearby Alsea Bay. The air is still.

I stroke the putt. As if pulled by a soup-can magnet, the ball rolls straight for the cup, for the jaws of victory, for the gentle reminder to my worthy young foe that, in the sea of life, I'm more than just some forty-something flounder. Then suddenly, inexplicably, the ball veers left like a sickly crab and dies two feet away.

Huh?

We tie.

But after a handshake and a maple bar, I realize that we have come a long way, father and son—much farther than seven miles. We have shared a sunrise, something we've rarely done. We have made a memory that may be told around beach fires for years to come.

"You know I purposely missed the last putt."

"No way, Dad."

"Sure. You actually didn't think I wanted to *beat* you, did you?"

Above all, we have taken dead aim and hit life's real target, which has nothing to do with swinging a golf club and everything to do with seizing a moment.

No, I realize as the incoming tide erases our footsteps on the beach, we don't tie.

We win.

"Friendship is the greatest of worldly goods."
—C. S. LEWIS

19

GOLFING TERMS YOU NEED TO KNOW

Ace: a hole in one.

Address: the position of the body as you stand to hit the ball. Also known as the stance or setup.

Alignment: the way you have lined up your body, shoulders, and feet before you start the backswing.

Approach shot: a shot meant to reach the green.

Apron: the fringe of grass ringing the green, but not cut as fine as the green.

Away: The "away ball" is the ball farthest from the hole, and golf convention says that ball should be played first.

Banana ball: a ball that curves off to the right (for right-handed players) in a banana-shaped trajectory.

Barkie: when your ball hits any part of a tree but you still complete the hole with a par.

Beach: any sand bunker.

Best ball: a competition where an individual or team competes to earn the best net score on a hole.

Birdie: to finish the hole in one shot less than par.

Bird nest: a ball that lands in the thick rough and lies like an egg surrounded by deep grass.

Bogey: to finish the hole in one shot more than par. Double- or triple-bogeys are two or three shots over par, respectively.

Bump and run: a chip shot that lands in front of the target and rolls toward the hole.

Bunker: a hollow area filled with sand. Also known as a sand trap or trap.

Carry: The distance a ball travels from where it was struck to where it first strikes the ground. On some holes, shots must carry one hundred to two hundred yards to stay in bounds.

Chili-dip: to hit the ground before the ball when attempting to chip, resulting in an errant, weak lofted shot.

Chip and run: a low trajectory shot near the green in which the roll is considerably longer than the carry.

Chip shot: a short, running iron shot played from the area surrounding the green.

Divot: a shot that takes a clump of grass with it. A good divot must start where the ball lies.

Dogleg: a fairway that bends at an angle, either to the right or left, leading to the green. A "dogleg right" or a "dogleg left" refers to hole that is a bit crooked, like a dog's leg.

Drive: the first shot made from a tee on par-4s and par-5s.

Driving range: an area where golfers can practice their shots; usually includes a putting green and chipping area. A good place to try hitting a golf ball.

Drop: bringing the ball back into play after striking the last shot out of bounds or into a water hazard. The ball is released from an outstretched arm held at shoulder height.

Eagle: to finish the hole two less than par. For instance, a hole-in-one on a par-3 would also be an eagle. A *double eagle* is the rarest shot of all—a hole-in-one on a par-4 or sinking the second shot on a par-5.

Fairway: the area of closely mowed grass running from the tee boxes to the green.

Fat: describes a shot where the club strikes the ground behind the ball, cutting down on its distance. Also known as hitting the ball heavy or chili-dipping the ball.

Flagstick: also known as the pin, the flagstick stands in the golf hole and is removed for putting.

Follow-through: where the club finishes at the end of the swing.

Fore: a warning cry to persons ahead who might be hit by your shot.

Fried egg: when a ball lies half-covered in a sand crater like a sunny-side-up egg.

Gallery: spectators who watch a golf tournament.

Gimme: When a shot comes so close to the hole, your opponent may assume that only one stroke would be required to putt it in and offers to allow you to simply count that stroke and pick the ball up. This often occurs when the ball is twenty inches or less from the hole.

Golf clubs: usually found in three different ways: private clubs with an initiation fee and monthly dues; semiprivate clubs are private clubs that allow the public to play at a daily rate: municipal courses are usually city-owned courses open to the public.

Green: the close-cropped putting surface, usually cut to a height of 3/16 of an inch.

Grip: refers to the position of the hands as they hold the club.

Hazard: any natural or artificial part of the course that can trap or block your ball from a clear shot, such as trees, tall grass, sand traps, bunkers, streams, lakes, water holes, ditches, etc.

Hole in one: to put the tee shot on a par-3 hole into the hole. Also known as an ace, holes-in-one happen around once in every twelve thousand shots.

Honors: the right to play first at the start of any hole. Determined by lot or agreement on the first hole, honors goes thereafter to the player with the lowest score.

Hook: a shot that curves to the left. A duck hook is a shot that takes a severe curve to the left. Also known as a snap hook, dive hook, or blue darter.

Lie: where the ball is resting, waiting to be hit. Lies can be good, and they can be atrocious, but the better the lie, the better chance of a good shot.

Load and unload: refers to the cocking and uncocking of the wrists.

Long-iron shots: shots taken with the 2-, 3-, and 4-irons that travel further but are more difficult to control.

Mulligan: when you are allowed to replay a shot (usually off the tee). Not allowed in an official scoring game.

Oversized heads: most woods and irons are built with oversized heads, which makes them more forgiving.

Par: the number of strokes that it takes a good golfer to score on a hole. Most courses are par-72 for eighteen holes.

Provisional ball: the playing of a second ball from the same place as the first because the player is unsure if the first shot landed out of bounds or is lost.

Putt: a rolling shot on the green that hopefully ends in the hole.

Rhythm: the harmonious movement in the swing with a regular and repeating pattern.

Rough: the sides of the fairway and golf hole in which the grass is allowed to grow higher. The ball is more difficult to hit when embedded in grass.

Sandy: when you make par on a hole after landing in a sand hazard.

Shanking: a shot that flies off at right angles, caused by hitting the ball with the club shank instead of the face.

Short-iron shots: shots taken with the 7-, 8-, and 9-irons, usually as approach shots to the green.

Slice: a shot that severely curves to the right, usually out of bounds. A fade is a shot that curves slightly to the right.

Square: a term with several uses in golf. It may refer to the clubface when it is positioned at right angles to the target line; to the stance when a line drawn across the heels is parallel to the target line; or to center-faced contact with the ball when it is struck.

Snowman: to score an eight on a hole.

Spikeless shoes: very few clubs allow golf shoes with metal spikes; today's shoes must have plastic cleats or molded outsoles.

Tempo: the rate of the swing, from slow to fast. Most swings take two seconds from takeaway to finish.

Three-quarter swing: when the hands are swung to 11:00 A.M. (full cocked in backswing) and to 1:00 P.M. on the follow-through.

Woods: refers to the driver, 3-wood, 5-wood clubs, etc. The clubheads are made out of composite materials, but were originally made with wood; hence the term "woods."

Worm burner: a shot that rolls along the ground.

Yips: when you miss simple putts or chips because of nerves.

RESOURCES

Wally Armstrong has written a number of golf books that integrate golf and faith and life.

In His Grip (with Jim Sheard)
Playing the Game (with Jim Sheard)
Finishing the Course (with Jim Sheard)
The Heart of a Golfer (with Frank Martin)

Wally's creative training tools, videotapes, DVDs, and other golf products can be purchased through these Web sites:
www.wallysworldofgolf.com
www.legacy-golf.com
Also on these sites you may gain information on Wally's golf clinics and speaking engagements.

To contact Wally personally:

Gator Golf Enterprises
P.O. Box 941911
Maitland, FL 32794
Ph 407-644-3398
Fx 407-644-9093

E-mail: snagwally@cfl.rr.com

ACKNOWLEDGMENTS

It would be impossible to thank all those who made this book possible. But I would like to honor those who played a great role in my life as a junior golfer, teacher, and writer.

Special thanks to my father, Walter Jr., and my mother, Lois, for starting me out in this wonderful game with Mom's hand-me-down ladies Hazel Hickson clubs.

Fred Keesling (golf professional at Fort Benjamin Harrison Golf Club) for giving me my first lesson as a junior golfer.

Jack Keesling (golf professional at Indian Lake Country Club and Old Oakland Golf Club) for his passion to reach young people with the spirit of the game but more importantly with the gospel.

Dr. Joe Miller for his great friendship and modeling the true spirit of the game to me.

Duke Dupree for mentoring me and instilling in me a love for practicing all the creative shots in the game.

Reno Newburg, my high school golf coach and who stuck with me during some difficult times of adjustment and for believing in me.

Conrad Rehling (golf professional University of Florida golf course), who took me under his wings during my master's degree and taught me how to teach golf in fun and creative ways.

Scott and Blake, my two fantastic sons who blessed me with many wonderful moments of joy as we did our numerous wild and crazy junior golf clinics together.

Mike Yorkey for his tremendous steadfastness in putting this book together in such a wonderful way.

Gary Terashita for believing in the concept of this book but more importantly the vision of how this book will enrich the lives of parents and their children.